LAYING DOWN
THE LAW

LAYING DOWN THE LAW

Mysticism, Fetishism, and the
American Legal Mind

PIERRE SCHLAG

NEW YORK UNIVERSITY PRESS
New York and London

NEW YORK UNIVERSITY PRESS
New York and London

© 1996 by New York University

Frontis: The Image Bank/Petrified Collection.

Library of Congress Cataloging-in-Publication Data
Schlag, Pierre.
Laying down the law : mysticism, fetishism, and the American legal
mind / Pierre Schlag.
p.   cm.
Includes bibliographical references and index.
ISBN 0-8147-8053-9 (alk. paper)
1. Law—Philosophy—Study and teaching—United States.
2. Jurisprudence—Study and teaching—United States.   I. Title.
KF380.S32   1996
340'.1—dc20   96-27348
CIP

New York University Press books are printed on acid-free paper,
and their binding materials are chosen for strength and durability.

Manufactured in the United States of America

10 9 8 7 6 5 4 3 2 1

For Nicolai, Kate, and Zoe

CONTENTS

ACKNOWLEDGMENTS

This book contains essays that were written between 1987 and 1995. They have been previously published in slightly different form. They are included here with permission from the law reviews. This includes "This Could Be Your Culture—Junk Speech in a Time of Decadence," 109 *Harvard Law Review* (1996); "Anti-Intellectualism," 16 *Cardozo Law Review* 1111 (1995); "Values," 6 *Yale Journal of Law of the Humanities* 195 (1994); "How to Do Things with the First Amendment," 64 *Colorado Law Review* 1095 (1993) "Pre-figuration and Evaluation," 80 *California Law Review* 965 (1992); "Normative and Nowhere to Go," 43 *Stanford Law Review* 167 (1990); "Contradiction and Denial," 87 *Michigan Law Review* 1216 (1989); "Fish v. Zapp: The Case of the Relatively Autonomous Self," 76 *Georgetown Law Review* 37 (1988).

Many people commented on drafts, gave suggestions, criticisms, and more. Some helped with resources, others with conversation. For this help, I would like to thank Dave Boerner, Jean Braucher, Craig Callen, Paul Campos, David Carlson, David Clark, Richard Collins, Richard Delgado, Syd DeLong, David Eason, Rebecca French, Steve Heyman, Susan Kezele, Deborah

Maranville, Bob Menanteaux, John Mitchell, Bob Nagel, Chris Rideout, Ed Rubin, Jack Schlegel, David Skover, Steve Smith, Steve Winter, and Andy Walkover. Special thanks to Richard Delgado and Jean Stefancic, who encouraged me to put the book together.

I

INTRODUCTION

ONE

This Could Be Your Culture

Law is not doing well currently. The lay public, never overly fond of lawyers to begin with, seems to be especially annoyed with them now. Even lawyers do not like each other very much: they accuse each other of greediness, of commercialism, of lack of collegiality. In the legal academy, things are not much better. Demoralization rules. Legal thinkers have no respect for judges. Judges have no respect for legal academics. And all but the most devout seem repulsed by the imperious overweening advent of America's overwrought legalism.

There are many reasons for this. One of them is that when it comes to what is called "law," there may not be much to admire. There is no method, no great learning, no illuminating texts, no real craft, no art worthy of the name. There are only great problems. And ironically, rather than recognizing these great problems, American legal thought is largely devoted to their denial. Indeed, for the past several generations, American legal thinkers have done little but *celebrate* what they variously call "law." To some, this claim may seem counterintuitive. Indeed, it might be countered

Note: A version of this essay was presented at a workshop, "The Indeterminacy of Social Intergration," December 2, 1995, at the Internationales Forschungszentrum Kulturwissenchaften, Vienna, Austria.

3

that American legal thinkers are relentlessly critical of law. In a sense (a very limited sense), this objection is right. What the objection misses, however, is that criticism of law is almost always in the service of the law itself. And this is so in two ways. First, the critical gesture is almost always nested in a larger disciplinary project aimed at the maintenance, perfection, or reform of the law. The critical gesture is almost always beholden not merely to a project of redemption, but more specifically, to a project of redemption *for law*. Second, inasmuch as the critical gesture rarely departs from legal aesthetics, the performance of this critical gesture is in effect a tacit endorsement of the law itself, a reassertion of the primacy of the legal mind. The critical moment in American law thus tends to be short and shallow. By and large, the enterprise of American legal thought has been dedicated to the admiration, celebration, praise, extension, preservation, and perfection of law.

Indeed, if one can summarize contemporary American legal thought, it has been one huge contest in which the various participants have tried to capture "law" for their own immensely admirable purposes: justice, efficiency, order, moral perfection, liberation, literary self-gratification, and the like. It has been one huge contest in which the goal has been to make law track with various academicized versions of the admirable.

Ronald Dworkin, perhaps America's leading jurisprudential thinker, is clearly on to something when he writes that the practice of law is to *make itself the best it can be*. What he is clearly on to, however, is not the practice of law. Indeed, for anyone who cares to look, making the law the best it can be *is most definitely not* a dominant characteristic of the practice of law. It *is*, however, very much the practice of being a legal academic.

The economic logic of such inflationary rhetoric is not difficult to fathom: full employment for lawyers. Nor is it difficult to uncover the psychological logic at work here either: it is pleasing to think pleasing things about one's chosen profession. And, of course, it is even more pleasing to think truly grandiose things about one's chosen profession.

Still, after a while all this self-congratulatory rhetoric can become dispiritingly self-referential. It can seem a bit unseemly, not to mention improbable. Indeed, paeans to "law" are increasingly preposterous—verging on self-parody. Hence, it is that, in the work of a leading legal thinker, the imperious bureaucratic droning of the O'Connor-Kennedy-Souter opinion in *Planned Parenthood v. Casey* is somehow rendered worthy of comparison to the thinking of Plato and Aristotle.[1] This sort of grandiose gesture, as improbable as it is, has nonetheless become routine in the American legal academy. Again, it is Ronald Dworkin who captures its spiritual essence:

> What is law? . . . Law's empire is defined by attitude, not territory or process. . . . It is an interpretive, self-reflective attitude addressed to politics in the broadest sense. Law's attitude is constructive: it aims to lay principle over practice to show the best route to a better future, keeping the right faith with the past.[2]

When confronted with something like this, one wants to ask: *Just what "law" is it that you are talking about here?* Are you talking about anything more than the law of the legal theory workshop? Do you *really* mean to refer by this term "law" to what judges, lawyers, clients, felons, legislators, or citizens might be referring to when they use the term "law"?

One wants to ask these ontological questions. One wants to ask these questions because it seems that most of these legal thinkers seek to induce a certain conflation between what they celebrate as "law" and the ugly bureaucratic noise that grinds daily in the nation's courts, legislatures, and agencies. It is, of course, possible that they do not intend such a conflation. Perhaps, when they speak of "the law" they do not mean to refer to the bureaucratic noise of our courts, legislatures, and agencies. Perhaps they are speaking of a different "law"—one which only they have seen. But if so, they owe it to us to say so, straightforwardly. And the likelihood is that they intend the conflation. If they do, then their unrestrained and at times self-indulgent celebrations of "law" are praises of raw bureaucratic power. They are speaking niceness to power.

There is nothing admirable in that.

There are noble moments in law. There are ignoble moments in law. It is difficult *intellectually* to identify their ratios and relations. But there is absolutely no reason to suppose that "the law" or the "extension of law" is necessarily or generally an admirable thing. To think that it is, is a category mistake.

It is a category mistake that those trained in law learn to make early and often—routinely, without thinking. In the world of law, this category mistake is represented not as a mistake at all, but as the obvious and undeniable truth. And so to rid oneself of this category mistake is no easy task. Among other things, this book is an attempt to explore the construction of this category mistake. It is an attempt to arrive at a point, where the urge to legislate reality dissolves—where one can lay down the law.

The essays in this book are thus a kind of journey—an attempt to understand the character and the identity of American law and legal thought. At some point, this journey produces something that was not expected at its inception. The endpoint of this journey is a point at which the law (the idea of law) no longer seems possible. It no longer seems possible to *believe in* "the law."

This realization, of course, does not abate the pressing need for law. The need continues. The gods may have left the temple, but the people wish to continue their worship.

This is a cultural predicament described by Nietzsche. For Nietzsche, the death of God meant not only that the Judeo-Christian God was dead, but that the entire metaphysics implicated in his reign died as well. Hence, once God died, so did all the other God-substitutes (reason, law, morality) that might have been or might yet be enshrined in his metaphysical place. We are living this cultural predicament. We are the ones who live in a culture in which it is no longer possible to believe in the law and not yet possible not to believe in the law.

* * *

Judges, lawyers, and legal academics and all others who "do law" must live this paradox. Those who understand themselves to be doing law must act as if they believed in the law, in its self-representations, and in its promises to effectuate its claimed ends. But, of course, to any person who is not busy doing law, the claims of law often seem quite preposterous, simply not to be believed. Consider the kinds of things that American law asks judges, lawyers, law teachers, and law students to believe:

That law is open and generally known to the public;

That human action generally comports with Newtonian conceptions of causation;

That the legislative or bureaucratic actions of collective bodies, like legislatures, can be analyzed in terms of the human attribute of intention;

That there are determinative methods for deciding whether a case is "correctly decided";

That human states of mind comport with a schema that conveniently breaks down into the cognitive states known as "intent," "recklessness," and negligence."

Then, too, law demands the belief that there exists some technique or faculty that enables decisionmakers to balance incommensurable goods (for example, the flag against the First Amendment) in order to reach correct outcomes. Law demands the belief that such balancing decisions are intersubjectively valid among a sufficiently large community (namely, citizens) or a sufficiently enlightened community (namely, the legal profession) that the decisions are legitimate.

Among the intellectual elites, it takes a special mind to believe such things. It takes a legal mind, one that can be perfected through years of arduous training. Acquiring a legal mind, however, is not without its psychic costs. Imagine, for a moment, a person who believed all of the above not only in his or her capacity as a law student or an appellate advocate or a sitting judge or a professing academic, but as a whole person. Imagine someone, in other words, who took the empirical, aesthetic, and metaphysical representations of Supreme Court opinions as valid descriptions of social life. We would be dealing, I think, with something on the brink of madness.

To varying degrees, first-year law students are invited to participate in this madness. They are led to believe, for instance, that the doctrine of proximate cause is valid social theory. In the realm of the First Amendment, they are prompted to believe that speech is very often weightless — noncoercive, nonmanipulative, and nonperformative. They are invited to believe these things not simply as law, but as valid descriptions of the social reality to which the law will be applied.

Although this kind of true belief endures in some law students, most, no doubt, eventually shed this untroubled faith. Students come to understand that these beliefs are germane to the enterprise of law. They are views one must hold or pretend to hold to do law. The law student realizes that it would be error to suppose that these are valid descriptions of social reality. Instead, the law student comes to believe that these views are valid descriptions of reality for the limited purpose of doing law. This mind-set is the beginning of a well-known and recursive disjunction:

Speech Act	Formal Precinct	Informal Precinct
What the law student says	in class	outside of class
What the law professor says	in class	in the faculty lounge
What the judge says to counsel	in open court	in chambers
What the conference panelist says	at the podium during the panel	in the hall after the panel

This disjunction embodies a divided state of belief. This state of belief embraces both belief and disbelief. Hence, to do law, the legal actor must not only profess that the beliefs he or she holds are valid descriptions of the relevant social reality, but that they are his or her own.[3] An appellate or trial court advocate cannot reveal to the judge or the jury what may well be the informal truth of the matter. He or she cannot ever say, "Look, I'm just a lawyer, and I think the argument I am making is a pretty good one, but of course, I don't believe it for one second." On the contrary, the advocate must profess belief (even if it is not there).

To describe things this way foregrounds the sense of disjunction. This disjunction can appear in different guises more or less acute, more or less problematic. Hence, at times it assumes a material form: for instance, it emerges as a discordance between the law-talk of formal precincts (the classroom, the podium, the courtroom) and the law-talk of the informal precincts (the hallway, the faculty lounge, the judge's chambers). At other times, it appears as a dissonance between "law in action" and "law in the books." At still other times, the disjunction is expressed as a formalized distinction between the so-called internal and external perspectives.[4]

The disjunction can emerge in many other forms. But the important point is that, however manifested or expressed, this disjunction remains a crucial aspect of the ontology of American law: it does not go away.

This is a disjunction which a person "doing law" must at the same time recognize and yet deny. Much of American jurisprudence can be understood as a collection of strategies to negotiate the conflicting demands of this disjunction. And there is something tragic about this because many of the strategies for dealing with this disjunction are not terribly satisfactory. We may sketch some of these strategies here.

One can, of course, recognize the disjunction and deny its force. This path leads either to formalism or opportunism (neither term is pejorative here). On the formalist side, one simply denies any social referent that fails to conform to law. One understands law to be fully effective in describing and constituting the objects that it purports to regulate. When one is doing law, there is nothing else. What seems objectionable about this approach (from an external standpoint) is its imperialism, its mechanistic self-confidence, its violent and arrogant disregard of other forms of life. On the opportunist side, by contrast, one simply gives up on any transcendental role for law understanding implicitly that law is a rhetoric, a lie, a useful way to get things done. What seems objectionable about this approach (from an external standpoint) is its amorality, or even immorality.

One can also recognize the disjunction and fail to deny it. This path leads to legal nihilism (not a pejorative term here). This option is a plausible orientation for someone who studies rather than does law or someone who is talking about law in an informal precinct. It is not plausible, however, for someone who is doing law in a formal precinct. What seems objectionable about this approach (from an external standpoint) is that, for those who are doing law, this approach cannot be lived—at least not authentically.

Most American legal thinkers reject the extremes of formalism, opportunism, and nihilism. Instead, their main stratagem lies in a redemptive view. This disjunction is expressed in a time-line formatted in the great image of progress: the present is inadequate, but the future shows great promise. The redemptive view admits the disjunction between the legal and the social, the ideal and the real, and the normative and the descriptive, but holds that, in time, the former can still be perfected and used to regulate, organize, and constitute the latter. The redemptive view thus recognizes and denies the disjunction. The recognition lies in an admission of a disjunction in the present. The denial operates through a presumption that normative prescription can eventually bridge the gap.

This view is expressed, at times, in such various perfectionist jurisprudences as realist policy analysis, critical legal studies, neopragmatism, and law and economics. All these schools of thought acknowledge that law is not what it represents itself to be. But in each case, there is also a redemptive promise that the law can be made to conform to its ideal self-representations.

All of this perfectionist jurisprudence presupposes, of course, that the ideal representations of the law—all these normative arguments consisting of lofty hopes, noble values, sound policies, appealing principles, well-crafted doctrines—somehow regulate the actual uses made of law by litigants, lawyers, and judges. It is not easy to believe such things, at least not for those legal thinkers who are acquainted with the coercion, wheedling, needling, harassment, and other rude and crude practices of lawyers.[5] How then can legal thinkers maintain the faith that law is regulative of its actual social uses? This is a difficult question.

Certainly, it is not an inconceivable notion that the ideal representations of law are regulative of law's uses. On the contrary, some such notion has been conceived over and over again throughout the history of American legal thought. It has been, and still is, a tacit background presumption of analytical jurisprudence, normative legal theory, and doctrinal analysis. Yet, once one begins to question whether the ideal representations of law are regulative of its uses, the faithful affirmation of the presumption is a complete nonstarter. What is needed instead is an argument to buttress the view that the ideal representations of law are regulative of law's ruder and cruder uses.

And here, one should note that the philosophical argument that it is *necessary* to make such a presumption is of no moment whatsoever. This argument typically goes something as follows: to have law at all, one must presuppose that law is indeed regulative of its own deployment. It may be true that this presupposition is a precondition for "law" properly so-called. And it may be true that, unless the precondition holds, we do not have law properly so-called. But even if this is true, it cannot establish that in any given social context, the law invoked by various social actors *is* indeed law properly so-called. Nor does the point change, however much those social actors may desire that their law be law properly so-called. This philosophical argument about the necessary internal conceptual structure of law as regulative is neither here nor there when the question is precisely whether, in given social practice, the invocation of law is regulative of its uses or not. In this context, the presumption quite simply begs the question.

It is not easy to believe that the ideal representations of law are regulative of its uses. Not only must one believe that the crucial relation is that of regulation, but one must believe as well that the ideal respresentations of law are distinct from their uses.

These presumptions are made by all manner of legal thinkers in the pursuit of their own jurisprudential projects. How is their faith sustained?

The answer is that law erases its own doubts, negates its own inadequacies, denies its own internal instability. This is accomplished through acts of violence that destroy the various potentialities of law and transform it into an objective, stable, univocal, monistic self-representation. These acts of destruction are visited internally within the law and externally as well, destroying the worlds imagined, planned, and established by those who lose out in the legal process.[6] This destruction usually cannot be admitted, but must instead be performed through operations and mechanisms that bear more respectable, more solemn, more somber names.

But, as solemn and somber as law may be, it has been very difficult for law to be serious. If one considers recent contributions to jurisprudence, what is most striking is their utter improbability. Hence, it is, we are told,

That legal formalism may be intellectually exhausted, but sound policy analysis can infuse it with new life;[7]

That the professionalism of the American lawyer is lost, but

he or she can still find rewarding work in a small law firm
environment;[8]

That Supreme Court opinions are written by clerks and read
like C.F.R., but that somehow law is still a kind of literature
worthy of comparison to the works of Plato or Aristotle;[9]

That there was a golden age of law (tentatively identified as
1958) to which we can return despite the fact that the
doctrinal dreck produced by this jurisprudence is precisely
what we are complaining about now.[10]

And so on.

Perhaps this lack of seriousness has always been there.[11] It certainly gives pause to recognize that in the late nineteenth century,
during the professionalization of the American law school (the
Langdellian years), law was considered a "science," cases considered "specimens," and law libraries were "laboratories." In
America, such explicit claims to scientific status have now been
largely dropped, though the old forms continue to rule from the
grave. In the years that followed Langdell, legal thinkers have
offered law review parades of pleasing normative fantasies and
detailed games of acute self-referential legalism. This pleasing
normative fantasy they have called "responsible scholarship." The
acute self-referential legalism they have called "real law." At certain times (recently, for instance) we have been unlucky enough
to have had both at once: a traditional legal-process fetishism
combined with unrestrained normative messianism.

II

THERE OUGHT
TO BE A LAW

TWO

Normative and Nowhere to Go

In many American law schools, one of the most revealing sites is the faculty lounge. A great deal of important information concerning the intellectual, political, and social character of a law school can be gleaned from the observation of this particular space and its characteristic transactions.

In many cases, the ethos of the institution can almost be read off from the decor. Is the lounge comfortable? Classy? Trendy? Functional? Shabby? What pictures adorn the wall? The framers, the donors, the elders? Is the lounge organized in several distinct spaces permitting several simultaneous gatherings of the faculty—or is there a central table, a central sitting area?

Then, too, one can learn a great deal from watching the behavior of the faculty members in the lounge. Who comes in? Who never comes in? Who leaves when who else comes in? Who talks? Who doesn't? What do they talk about? What do they never talk about? It is in the faculty lounge that basic patterns of law school faculty life are most openly manifested and read off.

Once, I walked into the faculty lounge, and a colleague asked me for what could well have been the six hundred and thirty-fifth time,

"What do you think the court should do? What should they do? What would you do?"

It was one time too many.

There is nothing quite like the exhilarating experience that comes from reading a provocative new piece of legal thought. Of course, at some point this exhilaration will give way to ennui as the new piece of legal thought unravels, ultimately to be classified as yet another possibly clever, perhaps thoughtful, but nonetheless utterly failed contribution. One characteristic feature of our own postmodern condition is the breakneck speed at which the second experience succeeds the first. From exhilaration to failure, the distance has been reduced to a couple of sentences.

Take the 1980s, for instance. Last I remember, it was 1979 and I was beginning my career. I had these incredible utopian visions and these absolutely uncontrollable yearnings to prescribe these normative visions to large numbers of strangers. I tried to find suitable employment where I could indulge these uncontrollable prescriptive impulses. So I became a cabbie in New York City.[1] Sometime during my third week on the job, one of my fares told me that I'd never make the grade. Oh sure, he said, I was normative enough—downright utopian. But I had no political sense. My timing was off, way off—not just by a couple of street lights, but by entire centuries. He called me a "liberal humanist." I didn't know what this meant, but his unmistakably derisive tone indicated that it was not something I was supposed to like. So I quit—a failed cabby.

And I became a legal academic instead.[2] The possibilities for normative speculation seemed endless. I would write for the Warren Court . . . forever . . . and no one would dare call me on it. Yes. And I would write the great American utopian chain novel—each chapter more morally appealing than the last.[3] I would argue that in the future, we should all be *really* moral—for even more than fifteen minutes.

Things were going really well and really morally. I was a real normativo—deep into *norm-selection* and *norm-justification*. And then this guy—the same guy who interrupted my promising career as a taxi driver—showed up again, out of nowhere. Just like that, right in the middle of my text. No transition at all. In fact, here he is. And he's saying that he's a postmodernist now, and that he wants to continue my text. Imagine my embarrassment. I tell him that this is an outrageous provocation, a scandal. He agrees. I tell him in no uncertain terms that I am the author and that I won't stand for this behavior, and that neither will the reader, nor the AALS. He says that I sound like "the interpretive turn," and that the interpretive turn has already turned into footnotes.

So I tell him that if he's a postmodernist, he couldn't possibly have anything to contribute to morality or ethics or politics, and that therefore he doesn't belong in my text. "Not at all," he said. "Postmodernism is already in this text. Postmodernism is here to do the charts on the normative articles of the eighties." "The charts?" I said. "What do you think this is? Top-40 radio? You can't do that. Normative articles are not the top 10, you know."

THE TOP TEN

#10. Have a Nice (Really Elegant and Totally Abstract) Day

This type of normative legal thought, a holdover from the seventies, is still very popular today. Typically, it takes some truly wonderful normative value, like justice or liberty or equality or whatever, and then tries its damnedest to give the abstract value a content that is as determinate and concrete, and yet as encompassing, as possible. While not necessarily deductive in structure, this sort of thought typically suffers from the same problem found in deductive legal thought. That problem is that in the movement from the abstract to the concrete, the mediations between the two are either not to be found, or they are found to be utterly unconvincing.

For those who like abstract value talk but don't want to traffic in the concrete at all, there is another option, particularly useful for those scholars who have figured out what should be done— for example, we should all be *really* nice to each other—but haven't the foggiest idea of how we should go about doing it. The thing to do is to name what should be done in a way that makes it look like a normative value—something that has life, force, and direction. This is not so much reification as it is animism, but it really does work, too. A lot of work. The next step is to argue very pontifically, with whatever drama liberal humanism can still muster, that we should all do or be more like the normative value. This kind of talk is often vacuous, but given sufficient self-righteousness, pomposity, pseudo-sophistication, or status in institutional affiliation, no one will notice. What's more, this sort of thought doubles really well as a graduation speech.

Recently, many legal academics have come to recognize that this abstract value talk actually excludes many members of the audience. In the formal structure of its discourse, abstract value talk pre-scripts the answers to many politically controversial questions. This point has been made forcefully by feminist and critical legal studies scholars.[4] This negative point is right and important. Unfortunately, it has yielded a positive program that appears to, but in fact does not, follow (logically or politically, or strategically) from the negative one. To say that abstract value talk is illegitimately exclusionary in no way suggests that . . .

#9. We Should Talk and Talk and Talk about Talk and Just Keep on Talking

Given the rather obvious bankruptcy of abstract value talk, the talk-talk genre has become very popular recently. My guess is that this strategy was created by some legal academics circling over Chicago's O'Hare Airport waiting to land. The main point of this strategy is to make normative legal thought really small—so small that it will contribute next to nothing to legal discourse. For example, note that this strategy does not even talk in a new way: it simply argues in all the old ways that we should talk the new talk. It is the jurisprudence of the holding pattern. Variations on old/new talk include the following: We should talk . . .

more normatively
more contextually
more like economists
more like civic republicans
more like narrative
more like normal (doctrinal) science
more like pragmatists

or in that hopeful humanist way until we figure out what the hell we're doing up here 30,000 feet from Earth arguing about how we should land.

One interesting thing about the talk-talk genre is that its basic question, "How should we talk?" assumes that how we talk is somehow *our* choice—that we (you and I) are already intellectually and politically enabled to decide, one way or another. Such an assumption is routine and uncontroversial within the dominant tradition of contemporary normative legal thought—namely, the epiphenomenological tradition.

And yet one begins to suspect that epiphenomenology cannot be the whole story. One begins to suspect that the answers given to the question, "How should we talk?" may well have been already scripted by as-yet unarticulated answers to questions such as: On what or whose terms are we already talking? What is making us talk? And who or what gets to stop the talk? One might begin to have these suspicions when one recognizes that even though the prescriptions for how we should talk all seem to vary considerably (and never seem to get adopted), the process, the form, the rhetoric of the argumentation that supports these prescriptions stays pretty much the same.

Some people, of course, get impatient with all this talk. It's too process oriented. It seems too far removed from what they see as the rightful focus of our normative attention on "substance." For those who are unhappy with the ultra-mediated character of the talk-talk genre, there is the self-announcedly more "substantive" formula:

#8. X—Good/Y—Bad

This is an extremely old and venerable genre—but still very current today. It has classic conservative lines and is always in good taste. Examples of this sort of thought include the following:

> Rule of Law—good/Legal Realism—bad
> Civic Republicanism—good/Liberalism—bad
> Feminist Jurisprudence—good/Critical Legal Studies—bad

Not all normative legal thought is as simple or as transparent in its normative structure as the above genres suggest—though, of course, ... Sometimes, however, the normative structure of the thought is difficult to discern because it is better dissimulated. For instance, it just might be the case that . . .

#7. The Zeitgeist Is Going My Way

In this sort of thought, the author and the arguments subtly recede into the background of the text. This thought strives to efface the author. Instead, an impressive compendium of trends, thoughts and authorities drawn from (virtually) every discipline just happen to coincide (in the footnotes, of course) to support a text which, in turn, just happens to support the normative program of the author's choice. The great advantage of this form of normative thought is that the inexorable force of the entire culture appears to be supporting the author's favorite normative program. Not only is the culture behind the author every step of the way, footnote to footnote, but fortuity is on the author's side as well. Invariably, it will appear that the culture has already moved substantially down the author's preferred normative path. In this best of all possible worlds, what ought to be is already becoming so — every day in every way.

One signal difficulty with this sort of all-points meteorological report is that the zeitgeist generally doesn't fit very well in footnotes. Maybe it's because the text/footnote distinction is so relentlessly Cartesian in character and thus inhospitable to the Germanic dynamism of the zeitgeist. Or maybe it's because the zeitgeist just doesn't believe in fine print. Both of these are possibilities. My sense, however, is that the real problem is that the zeitgeist is simply un-American: it simply is not willing to think of itself as some supporting accessory to our individual projects.

In any case, it invariably turns out that in this kind of thought, significant parts of the zeitgeist seem to be left out. This sometimes creates problems for the author, but it is seldom a problem for the zeitgeist. On the contrary: the excluded portions of the zeitgeist are virtually guaranteed to feature in another work, typically one that takes a diametrically opposed normative stance.

One of the striking things about these meteorological zeitgeist reports is that they rarely seem to pick up on postmodern currents. Striking, but not exactly surprising: Normative legal thought is structured not to recognize these kinds of currents. Indeed, normative legal thought is always already launched in the sort of interpretive enterprise guaranteed to read postmodernism right off the charts. This, of course, brings us to yet another venerable form of normative legal thought, which is none other than . . .

#6. Postmodernist Shadow-Boxing

This form of legal thought is squarely within the liberal humanist tradition. It offers maximum opportunities for righteous self-declamation about the moral wonderfulness of normative legal thought, as well as the moral wonderfulness of its author. Likewise, it offers tremendous possibilities to "fight the good fight" by warning of the utter amorality and irreducible evil of any intellectual current critical of liberal humanism—including, quite topically, postmodernism.

Postmodernism questions the integrity, the coherence, and the actual identity of the humanist individual self—the knowing sort of self produced by Enlightenment epistemology and featured so often as the dominant self-image of the professional academic. For postmodernism, this humanist individual subject is a construction of texts, discourses, and institutions. The promise that this particular human agent would realize freedom, autonomy, etc., has turned out to be just so much Kant. And the humanist individual subject has turned out to be Dan Quayle. Indeed, for postmodernism, the humanist individual subject has now become one of the main disciplinary vehicles by which bureaucratic institutions stylize, construct, organize and police their clientele. To inhabit the rhetorical space of the humanist individual subject, is to be—like Dan Quayle—subject to a variety of bureaucratic monitoring practices that, quite paradoxically but very effectively, transform the human being into the intellectual and social equivalent of a doe staring into the headlights. Liberal humanist talk of freedom, autonomy, choice, and so on seems, at least in this context, greatly out of place.

For postmodernism, the production of intellectual work that participates—in theory or in practice—in the ideology of this individualist humanist self is at best normatively ambivalent. On the one hand, such work may help achieve some desirable concrete end; on the other, the very performance of such work reproduces precisely the form of thought, the very rhetoric by which bureaucratic institutional practices re-present, organize, and reproduce their own operations, their own performances as the choices of autonomous, rational agents. Accordingly, the participation of normative legal thought in this liberal humanist ideology has become, *in terms of the very best values liberal humanism has to offer, morally ambivalent, if not immoral.*

Normative legal thought as a local legal variant of liberal humanism has correctly understood that it, too, is targeted by postmodernism. And so very courageously, normative legal thought has met the challenge head-on. The very first move of normative legal thought has been to assume automatically, *as a matter of its own form*, that it is authored by and addressed to an autonomous, coherent, integrated, rational, originary self, receptive to moral argument through a medium of language that is itself weightless and neutral. In other words, no sooner does normative legal thought begin to address postmodernism than it rhetorically assumes into existence precisely the sort of individual humanist subject—the very sort of author and reader—that postmodernism calls into question.[5]

This, of course, is a really terrific move.[6] Indeed, once normative legal thought rhetorically populates the world with these individual humanist subjects, the rest of the rejoinder to postmodernism is child's play. If the world is always already populated by such autonomous rational, morally competent individual subjects, then postmodernism is a lunatic and immoral effort to silence our last best hope for doing good in the world. The conclusion then follows effortlessly: if postmodernists want to contribute something to law or legal thought, they should first develop a normative vision. Here liberal humanism courageously converges with the Thumper school of jurisprudence: "If you can't say anything nice, don't say anything at all."[7]

If all this sounds like a series of winning moves, that's because in a sense—in a very solipsistic sense—it is. This is one of the beauties of disciplinary solipsism: if you never allow "the other" (i.e., here postmodernism) the possibility of changing your consciousness, your thought patterns, your cognitive or affective disposition, your text, etc., then you will always already be able to defeat "the other." You will always already win. Solipsism really does work . . . it does a lot of work.[8] It has worked really well for a really long time in legal thought. But notice three things about solipsism. *First thing:* The routine assumption of disciplinary solipsism that it is in control of its own intellectual or rhetorical situation seems somewhat overstated. *Second thing:* It gets to be rather boring to repeat the same old moves. And boredom is not something to be ignored. It is not something to be trivialized. Boredom is the structure's way of telling you something. It's telling you, "Yoo hoo, over here — I'm the structure, and boy, do I have your life down pat." *Third thing:* If you really think you are a self-directing, autonomous, liberal humanist subject, you really do have to wonder why it is you just always happen to "choose" to repeat the same old boring moves.

So much for the top 10 of normative legal thought in the eighties. Now you may have noticed that there are only five entries in the top 10. That is because the rhetorical situation of normative legal thought is even more desperate than I had initially imagined. To be sure, one could add other entries to the list, but then the redundancy quotient would rise intolerably and things would become rather repetitive and boring.

But then again, that is precisely one of my points. And there is no point in overdoing it — normative legal thought is overdoing it all by itself, getting more repetitive all the time, asking "What should we do? What should the law be? What do you propose?" over and over again.

In fact, even as you read and even as I write, normative legal thought is busy urging us (you and me) to ask these very same questions of this very essay at this very moment. "What should we do? What's the point?" asks normative legal thought. "If normative legal thought isn't going anywhere, what should we do instead?" "What do you propose?" "What's the solution?" These familiar questions are usually asked in searching, serious, somber tones. There is no trace of irony in their articulation—no self-consciousness at all. It is as if the intellectual legitimacy, the political import, of the questions were themselves self-evident, beyond question. "Yes, yes—but what should we do? How do these observations help?" Usually, the questions are asked with such earnest, self-assured self-certainty that it is as if the body of knowledge that enables the questions to be stated in the first place were somehow outside the problem, outside the difficulty—already intellectually whole, already politically competent to provide the answers. "Right, right, but the question is, what should we do with all this?"

Now you'll notice that here the "What should we do?" is *an interruption*. It is an interruption posing as an origin. It poses as an origin in that it takes itself to be the original motivation for engaging in legal thought. And yet here, the "What should we do?" interrupts the process of trying to understand what enterprise we, as legal thinkers, are already engaged in. It interrupts the process of attempting to reveal the character of our disciplines and our practices as legal thinkers. "O.K., O.K., but how would such revelations help us decide what we should do?"

You'll notice that here (as elsewhere) normative legal thought has a very pressing and urgent tone. It wants to know right away what should be done. Right away. And true to its name, normative legal thought wants to engage right away in the enterprise of *norm-selection*. Normative legal thought wants to decide as quickly as possible which norm (which doctrine, which rule, which theory) should govern a particular activity.

The urgency of normative legal thought masks the narrowness—both intellectual and political—of the *norm-selection* enterprise. Indeed, to engage effectively—that is, successfully—in *norm-selection* implies choosing a norm that will not require significant alteration of the audience's belief system. Only those kinds of norms that already conform to the audience's belief system are likely to meet with any sort of wide-scale approval. It is thus no surprise that the ready-made conceptualization of the scholarly project as one of norm-selection is one that ends with the validation of the *norm-selection* and *norm-production* process of the audience.

Now, as intellectually stifling and politically narrow as the enterprise of *norm-selection* may be, it still offers legal thinkers *some* residual possibility of posing interesting philosophical, social, psychological, economic, or semiotic inquiries about law. Yet normative legal thought can't wait to shut down these intellectual and political openings as well. It cannot wait to envelop these inquiries in its own highly stylized form of *norm-justification*. Normative legal thought cannot wait to enlist epistemology, semiotics, social theory, or any other enterprise in its own ethical-moral argument structures about the right, the good, the useful, the efficient (or any of their doctrinally crystallized derivatives). It cannot wait to reduce worldviews, attitudes, demonstrations, provocations, and thought itself to norms. In short, it cannot wait to tell *you* (or somebody else) what to do.

In fact, normative legal thought is so much in a hurry that it will tell you what to do even though there is not the slightest chance that you might actually be in a position to do it. For instance, when was the last time *you* were in a position to put John Rawls's difference principle[9] into effect, or to restructure the doctrinal corpus of the first amendment? "In the future, we should . . ." When was the last time you were in a position to rule whether judges should become pragmatists, efficiency purveyors, civic republicans, or Hercules surrogates?

Normative legal thought doesn't seem overly concerned with such worldly questions about the character and the effectiveness of its own discourse. It just goes along and proposes, recommends, prescribes, solves, and resolves. Yet despite its obvious desire to have worldly effects, worldly consequences, normative legal thought remains seemingly unconcerned that for all practical purposes, its only consumers are legal academics and perhaps a few law students—persons who are virtually never in a position to put any of its wonderful normative advice into effect. The possibility that a significant number of judges might actually be reading significant quantities of this academic literature is undemonstrated and unlikely. The further possibility that judges might actually be persuaded by this academic literature to adopt a position not their own is even more undemonstrated and even more unlikely.[10]

If there's no one in charge at the other end of the line, why then is normative legal thought in such a hurry to get its message across? And why, particularly, is it always in such a hurry to repeat the same old boring moves? There is an edge to these questions. And the edge comes in part from the implicit assumption that normative legal thought is a kind of thought and that, as thought, it is in control of its own situation, its own form, its own rhetoric.

But it isn't so. If normative legal thought keeps repeating itself, and if it is incapable of understanding challenges to its own intellectual authority, that is because it is not simply or even fundamentally a kind of thought. Normative legal thought is in part a routine. It is the highly repetitive, cognitively entrenched, institutionally sanctioned, and politically enforced routine of the legal academy—a routine that silently keeps legal thought channeled within the same old cognitive and rhetorical matrices.[11] Like most routines, it has been so well internalized that it is repeated automatically, without thinking. And like most routines, it remains unseen and unobserved—which is why it is so powerful.[12] It is an aspect—a significant aspect—of the unnoticed and untroubled overarching epistemic economy within which (virtually) all contemporary legal thought is produced. In terms somewhat misleading but more familiar to legal thinkers, normative legal thought is the latest incarnation of the Langdellian legacy, the latest variation on formalism—*normative formalism.*

Normative legal thought, of course, does not consider itself a formalist enterprise. And from the normative perspective, indeed, it is not. From the normative perspective, the formalist character of normative thought is not visible.[13] The very *form* within which normative legal thought represents the world prevents it from recognizing its own formalism. *Normative formalism,* like other formalisms, is its own best self-defense. It is its own best self-defense in the sense that whenever normative legal thought is intellectually challenged, it *unconsciously* reestablishes in the very *form* of the intellectual struggle its own fundamental understanding of the agenda, the issues, the legitimate forms of argumentation, the criteria of failure and success, and so on.[14] Self-defense, of course, is what disciplinary solipsism is all about.[15]

Admittedly, as solipsistic enterprises go, normative legal thought is pretty nice—or, at least, it looks pretty nice. For instance, it's really nice to think that legal thinkers and legal actors are all self-directing, coherent, integrated, rational, originary selves who are engaged in a rational conversation aimed at resolving disagreement by resort to normative dialogue. It's really nice to think that political disagreements turn upon self-conscious commitments to different "values." It's nice to think that law and politics can be subservient to a grand conversation about who we think we should become.

It is all very nice. It is also absolutely unbelievable. What is more, the unbelievable character of normative legal thought is becoming increasingly evident. And as legal thinkers become increasingly aware of the fantastic character of normative legal thought, the enchantment of normative legal thought weakens and withers.

Here, I'm just trying to help this disenchantment process along. Of course, it's not as if this process requires a great deal of help. On the contrary, we are just this far [...] away from recognizing that contemporary normative legal thought is a particularly shallow language game: "language game" in the Wittgensteinian as well as in the ludic sense,[16] and "shallow" in the sense of ... well, shallow. The normative jurisprudential world, built of arguments upon arguments upon arguments—just hanging there on the threads of normative structures marked out with concepts like fairness, consent, oppression, neutrality, and policed by aesthetic criteria like coherence, consistency, certainty, elegance—is about to crash. More accurately, it has already crashed, and it is just a matter of time before the entire legal academy takes notice. Now, of course, it may take considerable time for the academy to notice.[17] Indeed, it is one of the vexations of the condition in the legal academy, as elsewhere, that various kinds of thought remain socially and institutionally operative (in fact dominant) long after their intellectual vitality has dissipated. And so it is with normative legal thought. It remains socially and institutionally operative within the legal academy, though it is a jurisprudential world that has already crashed. The significant question is when and how the legal academy will take notice.

In an attempt to help this process of recognition along, what follows is a capsule description of the degeneration/development of normative legal thought. This degeneration/development proceeds in, and can be understood as, an increasing awareness by normative legal thought of its own role and character. As this degeneration/development unfolds, the meanings, the identities, and the grammatical relations of recurring terms such as "thinker," "thought," and "normative" change as well.

To begin with, consider a crude but illustrative example. If I call something "justice," this means that this something (whatever it is) is a good thing and that you too will want to be in favor of that thing. It also means that, if you do not want to be in favor of that something, then you will want to find some principled reason why the something I have called "justice" is not justice. This game can be played with other terms like "oppression," "choice," "consent," and so on. What is truly wonderful about normative legal thought, then, is that it immediately compels people to take certain roughly predictable steps in the dialogic game: "You're evil." "No I'm not." And so on (except with more argumentative flourish).

Admittedly, normative legal thought is more complex than these examples would suggest, but nevertheless, its rhetorical situation and the point remain the same: what is becoming increasingly evident to many legal thinkers is that "justice" and "oppression" and "coercion" and "consent," etc., and the grammar accompanying this vocabulary are all part of a normative language game. It is important not to make too much of this recognition. Just because some legal enterprise becomes identified as a language game does not necessarily mean that the participants in the game will stop or lose interest in playing that language game.[18] The term "language game," after all, is not pejorative . . . (except, of course within certain select language games that make the expression pejorative.)

Still, something interesting occurs with the recognition that normative legal thought is a kind of language game. Legal thinkers become aware that normative legal thought is largely a performative enterprise[19]—one that uses normative words and normative grammars instrumentally to induce specific kinds of social action. While this recognition may be obnoxious for some unreconstructed normative thinkers who insist upon maintaining the pure, transcendent character of normative thought, most legal thinkers will readily accept and accommodate themselves to this recognition. Indeed, the notion that normative legal thought is instrumentally effective not because of any so-called "intrinsic" normative authenticity, but rather because of its rhetorical facility for manipulating the self-image, and thus the self, of the reader is something that most normative legal thinkers can readily accept. Few care *how* normative legal thought does its work, so long as it *does* work.

Of course, once it is widely recognized that normative legal thought is a technique of rhetorical manipulation, the recognition itself begins to produce certain performative effects. Once legal thinkers understand that the significance of the normative categories and the normative grammar is largely performative, they assume a new stance towards normative rhetoric. They see it as an instrumental vehicle for achieving their favorite political or moral ends.[20] Consequently, normative rhetoric becomes subject to rather intense pressure. For example, consider the normative word "freedom." This particular word has a certain exchange value in American legal discourse. It is well known, for instance, that at present, "freedom" of [. . .] enjoys a certain rhetorical advantage over "security" of [. . .]. That is to say, at present, "freedom" is rhetorically superior to "security."[21] As legal thinkers come to recognize this point, they try to associate "freedom" with their favorite values, leaving "security" as the word for competing or interfering values. Thus the exchange value of the "freedom" word rises in the rhetorical economy of legal thought. However, the rise in the exchange value of such normative words typically yields an inflationary spiral. Sooner or later everybody is using the "freedom" word. For a while, the political charm of the "freedom" word can survive accelerated circulation. The word remains important. It remains important because it remains performatively effective. It is perceived as a tool, a rhetorical lever. But precisely because the "freedom" word remains performatively effective, it is immediately pressed further into all sorts of instrumentalist enterprises, thereby further diffusing its constative significance. After a while, the "freedom" word doesn't mean much of anything. It isn't even a reliable rhetorical tool to get people to act, or to be or to say various things. On the contrary, everybody knows the trick: freedom's just another word for getting you to do something you don't want to do.

Now this linguistic metamorphosis is hardly limited to the "freedom" word. Rather, the linguistic devaluation affects the entire normative currency. In fact, it affects the entire grammar of normative legal thought. Hence, entire structures, entire complexes of normative legal thought, become increasingly vacuous—their purchase on the world, descriptive and regulatory, becomes

less and less credible. Even the performative value of these structures and complexes becomes weakened as legal thinkers come to
recognize that their constative significance has been devalued.

As the normative currency is devalued, the relation between
normative structures and complexes, on the one hand, and the
practices to which they ostensibly correspond, on the other, becomes weakened, attenuated. No longer is it possible to maintain
a naive idealism or materialism where normative conceptions
such as "justice," "liberty," "consent," or "community" either determine or are determined by the practices to which they ostensibly correspond. The language of determination, and even its
softer, more nuanced dialects, no longer provide an adequate
understanding of the situation of normative legal thought. Here,
the point is *not* that normative legal thought has now become
indeterminate, as opposed to some previous or possible state of
determinacy. Rather, the point is that determination is no longer
the appropriate frame of reference for charting the relation between normative legal thought and the practices it ostensibly
addresses.

It is at this point that the legal thinker recognizes that the
value (if any) of normative legal thought does not depend so
much on its relation to the practices it seeks to describe or govern.
It now becomes evident that the value (if any) of normative
legal thought depends on a decentered economy of bureaucratic
institutions and practices—such as those constituting and traversing the law school, the organized bar, the courts—that define
and represent their own operations, their own character, their
own performances, in the normative currency. Indeed, at this
point, normative legal thought takes on a completely different
character. It becomes the mode of discourse by which bureaucratic institutions and practices re-present themselves as subject
to the rational ethical-moral control of autonomous individuals
(*when indeed they are not*), just as normative legal thought constructs us (you and me) to think and act as if we were at the

center—in charge, so to speak—of our own normative legal thought (*when indeed we are not*). Normative legal thought can no longer be seen to govern, regulate, or even describe human activity.

In fact, as a further step in this degeneration/development, it now appears that it is very difficult to discern any significant difference between normative legal thought and the operation, performance, reproduction, and proliferation of bureaucratic practices and institutions. The two collapse into each other. At this point, normative legal thought has become the operation, performance, reproduction, and proliferation of bureaucratic practices and institutions.

Normative legal thought is effective—very effective—but not in any way it imagines itself to be. Its significance can no longer be in its specific prescriptions or conclusions (which are rarely adopted or even capable of being adopted). Normative legal thought—this form of thought so concerned with producing normatively desirable worldly effects—has, ironically, become its own self-referential end.[22] And that end is coextensive with the operation, performance, reproduction, and proliferation of bureaucratic practices and institutions.

Welcome to the crash. My sense is that when legal thinkers recognize that normative legal thought is an economy of self-referential instrumentalist rhetorical structures run from elsewhere and gradually seeping themselves of meaning, both constative and performative, playing this language game of normative legal thought will lose a great deal of its moral and intellectual cachet. It is one thing to understand oneself as engaged in a normative enterprise aimed at improving the moral or political or economic performance of the legal profession or the courts through normative argument. It is quite another to understand oneself as a bureaucratic vehicle for the proliferation of a mode of discourse (normative legal thought) that is coextensive with bureaucratic practice and institutional inertia. As self-images go, the latter is not really great. It is likely to lead to a certain degree of disenchantment. And this disenchantment is already well on its way.[23]

Now, one reaction a normative legal thinker might have to all this is that it is all perfectly horrible—and that we should all try to preserve our normative universe by using words more carefully and by arguing very morally against instrumentalism and the instrumentalization of law (and so on). But this argument misses the point again. This is history—not dialogue among disembodied Cartesian selves. And it doesn't do much good to make normative arguments against history—especially not if you keep misidentifying your own addressee, your agent of change, your subject. Unfortunately, that is precisely what normative legal thought keeps getting confused about. It keeps thinking that it is addressing some morally competent, well-intentioned individual who has his hands on the levers of power. The pervasiveness of this metaphysical confusion—its routine character within the legal academy—is precisely what engenders the more socially situated confusions of "liberal" and "progressive" legal academics as to whether or not the Warren Court is still sitting.[24]

All of this can seem funny. That's because it is funny. It is also deadly serious. It is deadly serious, because all this normative legal thought, as Robert Cover explained, takes place in a field of pain and death.[25] And in a very real sense, Cover was right. Yet as it takes place, normative legal thought is playing language games—utterly oblivious to the character of the language games it plays, and thus, utterly uninterested in considering its own rhetorical and political contributions (or lack thereof) to the field of pain and death. To be sure, normative legal thinkers are often genuinely concerned with reducing the pain and the death. However, the problem is not what normative legal thinkers do with normative legal thought, but what normative legal thought does with normative legal thinkers. What is missing in normative legal thought is any serious questioning, let alone tracing, of the relations that the practice, the rhetoric, the routine of normative legal thought have (or do not have) to the field of pain and death.

And there is a reason for that: normative legal thought misunderstands its own situation. Typically, normative legal thought understands itself to be outside the field of pain and death and in charge of organizing and policing that field. It is as if the *action* of normative legal thought could be separated from the *background* field of pain and death. This theatrical distinction is what allows normative legal thought its own self-important, self-righteous, self-image—its congratulatory sense of its own accomplishments and effectiveness.

All this self-congratulation works very nicely so long as normative legal thought continues to imagine itself as outside the field of pain and death and as having effects within that field.[26] Yet it is doubtful that this image can be maintained. It is not so much the case that normative legal thought has effects on the field of pain and death—at least not in the direct, originary way it imagines. Rather, it is more the case that normative legal thought *is* the pattern, *is* the operation of the bureaucratic distribution and the institutional allocation of the pain and the death.[27] And apart from the leftover ego-centered rationalist rhetoric of the eighteenth century, there is nothing at this point to suggest that legal thinkers are in control of normative legal thought.

The problem for legal thinkers is that the normative appeal of normative legal thought systematically turns attention away from recognizing that normative legal thought is grounded on an utterly unbelievable re-presentation of the field it claims to describe and regulate. The problem is that normative legal thought, rather than assisting in the understanding of present political and moral situations, stands in the way. It systematically reinscribes its own aesthetic—its own fantastic understanding of the political and moral scene.

Until normative legal thought begins to deal with its own paradoxical postmodern rhetorical situation, it will remain something of an irresponsible enterprise. *In its rhetorical structure,* it will continue to populate the legal academic world with individual humanist subjects who think themselves empowered Cartesian egos, but who are largely the manipulated constructions of bureaucratic practices—academic and otherwise.[28]

To the extent possible, it is important to avoid this kind of category mistake. For instance, it is important to understand that your automobile insurance adjuster is not simply some updated version of the eighteenth-century individual humanist subject. Even though the insurance adjuster will quite often engage you in normative talk—arguing with you about responsibility, fairness, fault, allocation of blame, adequacy of compensation, and the like—he is unlikely to be terribly receptive or susceptible to any authentic normative dialogue. His normative competence, his normative sensitivity, is scripted somewhere else. It is important to be clear about these things. The contemporary lawyer, for instance, may talk the normative rhetoric of the eighteenth-century individual humanist subject. But make no mistake: This normative or humanist rhetoric is very likely the unfolding of bureaucratic logic. The modern lawyer is very often a kind of meta-insurance adjuster. And that makes legal academics trainers of meta-insurance adjusters.

This is perhaps an unpleasant realization. One of the most important effects of normative legal thought is to intercede here so that legal academics do not have to confront this unpleasant realization. Normative legal thought allows legal academics to pretend that they are preparing law students to become Atticus Finch[29] while they are in fact training people who will enter the meta-insurance adjustment business.

For law students, this role confusion is unlikely to be very funny. It will get even less so upon their graduation—when they learn that Atticus Finch has been written out of the script. For legal academics, of course, it is a pleasant fantasy to think that they are teaching Atticus Finch. When the fantasy is over, it becomes one hell of a category mistake. And in the rude transition from the one to the other, Atticus Finch can quickly turn into Dan Quayle. In fact, if one trains law students to become Atticus Finch, they will likely end up as Dan Quayle—cognitively defenseless against the regimenting and monitoring practices of bureaucratic institutions. Atticus Finch, as admirable as he may be, has none of the cognitive or critical resources necessary to understand the duplicities of the bureaucratic networks within which we operate. Apart from the fantasies of the legal academy, there is no longer a place in America for a lawyer like Atticus Finch. There is nothing for him to do here—nothing he can do. He is a moral character in a world where the role of moral thought has become at best highly ambivalent, a normative thinker in a world where normative legal thought is already largely the bureaucratic logic of institutions.

But don't worry—be normative. My bet is that when normative legal thought takes note of the crash, it will argue against it—on normative grounds, of course.[30] The argument will be structured in terms of the determination of the epistemic by the normative. Or in simpler terms: "There is no crash . . . because to acknowledge a crash (in law) would bring about terrible social consequences, a loss of meaning, etc. . . . Therefore, there can't be any crash. Therefore, there isn't any crash." Another winning argument. Actually, the argument has already been made—in fact, several times. It's part of the routine. We can even pretend the citations are here. They are. Really. It's just a matter of time.[31]

This argument will likely be accompanied by great and moving efforts to revive normative legal thought through the teaching of ethics and morality.[32] What else? Actually, one other thing. Normative legal thought, this local offshoot of liberal humanism, can be expected to do its usual conservative collapse move, and to mourn, in a nostalgic sort of way, the passing of the normative world. "In the old days, when people were moral . . ."[33]

Now, other than these sorts of responses, it would be unrealistic to expect anything else of normative legal thought *at present.*

Normative legal thought simply does not possess the sort of cognitive or critical resources to recuperate from the crash.[34] From the perspective of normative legal thought, either the crash does not exist, or if it does, it is simply an unaccountable, inexplicable intellectual and cultural catastrophe. Indeed, in static terms, the existing categories, the existing grammar of normative legal thought, are utterly incapable of providing any sort of sophisticated account for the crash. Viewed dynamically, normative legal thought could conceivably begin to apprehend the crash and respond. But, of course, that's not where the energies of normative legal thought are dedicated. On the contrary. Normative legal thought, like liberal humanism more generally, is spending (virtually) all of its intellectual and psychic resources fueling a denial of the crash.

Liberal humanism and normative legal thought are both very good at denial.[35] They ought to be. They are the routine. They are in place. They are institutionally and cognitively embedded.

By way of example, consider the scholarly exchanges among normative legal thinkers. They all differ about all sorts of things. They differ about "important" issues such as what should be the appropriate mix of community, liberty, freedom, equality, empowerment, efficiency, etc. And while normative legal thinkers differ about these "important" normative issues, there is one thing that they all agree upon, over and over again ... without even having to think about it. What they all agree upon, in this implicit unexamined sort of way, is that they are all autonomous, rational, morally competent individuals who are having a meaningful, important, and effective discussion about how society or some subdivision thereof should be organized.

This pleasant fantasy is harmless enough, except that it reproduces legal academics and law students (and hence lawyers) in the image of humanist individual subjects. This, too, is a harmless self-indulgence, except that it provides instrumentalist bureaucracies with an absolutely marvelous and captivating rhetoric that defines, organizes, routinizes, and services their clientele. It's all really neat. 7–11 sells freedom (which you can find in their Slurpees). Pepsi brings you the downfall of the Berlin Wall. And normative legal thought guides the development of the law.

THREE

Values

Those who "do law" or who believe they "do law" engage in a great deal of normative talk—of prescriptions and justifications. In part this is understandable: other than the invocation of authority, it is principally normative argument that transforms the disparate threads of the legal materials into the formulation of a single authoritative norm—the last line of the judicial opinion that reads "judgment for the plaintiff . . . ," "judgment reversed . . . ," and so on.

Given the prevalence of normative talk in law, moral and ethical values feature prominently. As a result, law can easily seem to be an ethically and morally admirable enterprise. It is easy to believe that insofar as law is forever concerned with identifying and prescribing the good and the right, it is therefore itself good and right.

But that is a category mistake. It is very much like the category mistake that the young philosophy student makes about her philosophy professor. She comes to believe that insofar as her philosophy professor is forever concerned with ethical theory and moral problems, he must therefore be a very ethical and moral person. This is a category mistake. It is the same kind of category mistake that occurs with respect to the normative character of law. In fact, it even occurs with "values"—as argued below.

* * *

Justice, goodness, rightness, truth, fairness, efficiency, order, progress, freedom, equality, security, tolerance, neutrality, community, honesty, loyalty, convenience, clarity, precision, comprehensiveness, consistency, rationality, elegance, rigor. These are just some of the key political, ethical, and aesthetic values of contemporary American law.

Much of American legal thought is dedicated to the identification and classification of these values in terms of rank, intensity, scope, compatibility, and commensurability. These values are analyzed, clarified, systematized, reconciled, balanced, sacrificed, overcome, and overwhelmed. Their implications are traced. They are deployed to support or attack sundry agendas. They are used to justify, redeem, uplift, motivate, command, and defeat. They feature at all stages in legal arguments: in their origins, their frames, their development, and their terminus.

Throughout all these various uses of values, there is one thing that is not much talked about: the action of valuation, the generative history of values. What is missing is any historical recollection of how these particular values came to be values for us, individually and collectively. Instead, values stand as an autonomous realm: values are *severed* from their generative history, and their generative history is *effaced.* Indeed, ironically, values become values for us precisely through this process of severance and effacement. In American law, we can see this ongoing process of severance and effacement at work in two pervasive rhetorics, which I will call the *presentist rhetoric* and the *rhetoric of the romanticized past.*

In the presentist rhetoric, legal thinkers depict and deploy values as the unquestionable rhetorical origins, the ultimate animating agencies, and the discursive limits of legal conversations. "Justice requires . . . ," they say. "Equality requires . . . ," they say. In this kind of rhetoric, values become the self-evident starting points and grounds of legal conversations. In this jurisprudential world, it is at once impossible and beside the point to ask about the generative history of value or values. It is impossible because values are taken to be self-evidently self-grounding and it is presumed that participants in the legal conversation already take values to be the primary source of authority.

In the rhetoric of the romanticized past, the generative history of values is supplanted by a mythic and highly idealized rendition of the authorial moment—the moment at which values become accepted as values. In this rhetoric, generative history is reduced to discrete authorial moments. For instance, the authoring of values in American law is ascribed to mystical foundational moments (e.g., "1789"), to venerated authoritative texts (e.g., "The Constitution"), to politically revered authors (e.g., "The Framers"), or to the sophisticated constructions of moral and political philosophy (e.g., John Rawls's "original position").[1] These accounts of how values have become values for us are not histories. They are, rather, "reconstructions" wishfully projected back on a temporal or philosophical past to create the origins we presently desire our values to have. Typically the authors represented in these "reconstructions" are very much like the idealized representations we have of ourselves. They give "reasons." They engage in "dialogue" and "conversation." They are "deliberative." These "reconstructed" authors are, in short, instantiations of the rational, coherent, relatively autonomous subject of liberal thought.[2]

Both the presentist rhetoric and the rhetoric of the romanticized past succeed in severing values from their generative history and effacing that history. This ahistoricism is not a remediable conceptual defect in what we take to be values. Rather, it is constitutive of the aesthetic frame within which "values" emerge as values for us. It is through the severance and effacement of values from the valuing action and the valuing agencies that values become what they are for us: *abstract idealizations* cast as *context-transcendent, regulative grounds.*

Values are *grounds* to the extent that they are shared within a community and to the extent that they establish the shared identities and self-definitions that make dialogue and deliberation possible. Abstraction enables members of a community to bracket nonessential differences. The idealized character of values serves as a rhetorical medium to command at least minimal consensus and minimal reciprocal recognition among members of the community.

Values are *context-transcendent* to the extent that they enable judgment or evaluation in a variety of different situations and circumstances. The abstract character of values establishes the possibility of context-transcendence, while the idealized character of values legitimates abstraction from the concrete specifics of particular contexts.

Values are *regulative* to the extent that they control or at least influence outcomes. As regulative grounds, values serve to identify and circumscribe the possible rhetorical resources that can be used and the decisions that can be reached by a community or its members.

To describe values as context-transcendent, regulative grounds in this way is to give a fairly conventional account of values.[3] Indeed, it is a flattering account inasmuch as it accords a powerful and normatively pleasing place to values and value-talk. This account is consonant with many of the goods often associated with values and value-talk. It is consonant, for instance, with Martha Nussbaum's account of values.[4] Hence, when Nussbaum writes that the abstraction of values means "there is something very important that binds us, whether we feel like it or not," she is referring to the *regulative* character of values. When she says that the appeal to abstract values "is a way of stopping debate by saying that there is something unchanging out there," she is referring to the fact that values are *grounds*. When she writes "that there are ethical standards that are independent of the norms and traditions of a particular culture," she is appealing to the *context-transcendent* character of values. And when Martha Nussbaum writes that the appeal to abstract values "can help us to systematize our beliefs and preferences," she is recognizing that values play a very significant role in organizing our normative universe.[5]

Indeed, one may trace many of the good and valuable uses conventionally ascribed to values and value-talk to the character of values as context-transcendent, regulative grounds. What is more difficult and possibly more important to recognize is that the constitution of values as context-transcendent, regulative grounds also harbors danger. This danger is traceable to precisely the same constitutive characteristics that make values seem appealing, important, and powerful in the first place.

The danger is that one might be led to ascribe a rhetorically foundational status to values and value-talk. Given that values are context-transcendent, regulative grounds, one might easily come to believe that value-talk or value advocacy is, *a priori*, morally or politically significant. This seems reasonable, but it is a non sequitur. Simply because values are, in and of themselves, constructed so as to have moral or political consequences does not mean that they necessarily or even usually have those moral or political consequences. The recognition that values are constructed as context-transcendent, regulative grounds might seem to establish a relation between "values" and their contexts, but it does not. To understand the relations between "values" and the contexts in which they are invoked, one cannot look merely at how "values" are constructed. It is also necessary to examine the contexts in which the "values" are invoked. To understand this point is crucial. It is crucial because the context within which a value is invoked may well be constructed in such a way as to deny, diffuse, exhaust, or even reverse the moral or political charge of that value.

For example, Martha Nussbaum ascribes all sorts of virtuous uses to values and value-talk. She says:

> values are binding on us
> values limit and stop debate
> values are transcultural and enduring

values enable systematization of our preferences and commitments.[6]

Now one can certainly imagine contexts in which the effective
presence of cultural resources (i.e., "values") that are binding, that
help limit and stop debate, that transcend cultures, and that
enable systematization of preferences would be helpful or desirable. But one can also easily imagine contexts in which the
effective presence of such cultural resources (i.e., "values") would
be extremely unhelpful and undesirable.

If the binding, debate-stopping, culture-transcendent, and
preference-systematizing characteristics of "values" are considered
virtues, it is only because their context has been prefigured to
render them virtues. Indeed, in some contexts, these virtues
quickly become vices:

values are binding on us	values are authoritarian
values limit and stop debate	values are silencing
values are transcultural	values are totalizing
values enable systematization	values enable reductionism

The point here is that regardless of the particular constitutive
characteristics of a value, one cannot tell whether its use is salu-
tary without understanding how that value is used and in what
context. The moral or aesthetic consequences of the invocation
of a value cannot be discerned merely from an examination of the
constitutive characteristics of that value. Nor is this point merely
"academic." On the contrary: ours is a world where compassion
for AIDS victims can be used just as easily to sell clothing as to
elicit funding for medical research, a world where the value of
freedom implies at once the downfall of the Berlin Wall and the
imbibing of Pepsi.[7]

In order to conclude that the invocation of values or value-talk
has significant moral or aesthetic consequences, one would have
to know something about the *ontological status* of "values" in any

given context. Specifically, one would have to know whether, in any given context, the values exist in the mode of illusion, fantasy, image, idea, cognitive determination, linguistic inscription, cultural formation, biological given, objective reality, some other modality, or some combination of the above. (One would also have to know what hold any of these modalities have within the particular culture in which the values are invoked.) Similarly, in order to conclude that the invocation of values or value-talk has moral or aesthetic consequences, one would have to know something about the *performative role* values play in any given context: persuasive, disciplinary, coercive, rationalizing, justifying, shaming, organizing, some other role, or some combination of the above.

Nor does it do any good to restrict the object of inquiry, in the manner of some analytical moral philosophy and much American jurisprudence, to "proper" or "authentic" or "normal" uses of "values," leaving nonconforming uses to the disciplinary oblivion of some devalued site labeled "improper" or "inauthentic" or "aberrant." Such devices are familiar enough in American intellectual life. They are used over and over again to delimit the object of inquiry and to define intellectual jurisdiction in a way that will allow formalization of the field of investigation.[8] We know these devices by various names, including:

proper/improper
authentic/inauthentic
normal/aberrant
internal/external perspective
essential/contingent
pure/corrupt
serious/nonserious
langue/parole
structure/performance
theory/practice

That the intellectual jurisdiction and aesthetic configuration of many of our disciplines (including much analytical moral philosophy and American jurisprudence) is grounded on and delimited by such devices is not cause for confidence. Rather, it is reason to doubt the intellectual integrity of those disciplines.

Indeed, to say that a discipline will speak only about the "proper" uses of values, leaving "improper" uses to some degraded and unexamined realm, is to say that a discipline will only study the values it has defined into existence for itself. It is no doubt a fine thing for a discipline to devote itself to the study of its own posited creations (here, values), but this procedure is not without certain risks—risks of disciplinary solipsism. Once a discipline (like much analytical moral philosophy or American jurisprudence) dedicates itself to the study of its own posited creations, two questions become critically important. First, it becomes necessary to ask: What is the ontological status of the posited creations (here, values) studied by the discipline? Second, one needs to ask whether there are any interesting relations at all (and if so, which ones) between what those within the discipline call the posited creations (here, values) and human life generally.

So the questions remain: What is the ontological status of values in any given context? What is the performative role of values in any given context? In one sense, one would think that these questions would be of interest to those who are concerned with the moral efficacy of their own value-talk. Similarly, one would think that these questions would be of interest to those who are interested in what lawyers do.

But value-talk—whether in analytical moral philosophy or American jurisprudence—does not and cannot answer these questions. It cannot answer these questions because the very practice, the very plausibility of value-talk already presupposes an answer to these questions. What value-talk presupposes is that it is already constituted as an intellectually serious and morally efficacious enterprise (and so too, therefore, are its posited creations—values). Before one can indulge in such optimistic and self-congratulatory presuppositions, however, it is necessary to understand what values and value-talk are and how they are related in any given instance to social and legal practices.

The Ontological Status of Values

To describe values as *context-transcending, regulative grounds* does not establish or specify their ontological status; that is, this description does not establish or specify the manner or the modalities of being in which values are. Hence, as previously suggested, it does not establish whether values are in the mode of illusion, fantasy, image, idea, cognitive determination, linguistic inscription, cultural formation, biological given, objective reality, some other modality, or almost any combination of the above to varying degrees.

To say, as has been said here, that values are idealized abstractions or that they are context-transcending, regulative grounds does not answer the ontological question. One must remember that God, too, once was (and in some senses, still is) an idealized abstraction. He, too, once was (and in some senses, still is) regulative and context-transcending, indeed, the all-time ground for evaluation. But, of course, these attributions of essential traits to "God" do not, indeed cannot, establish in what manner of being he was (or is). In this respect, values are his pantheistic successors in interest. Values are like little divinities.[9] Like God, they serve as grounds or unquestioned origins. Like God, their invocation demands worship, reverence, and self-abnegation. Like God, they provide comfort and compensation for an otherwise degraded reality. Like God, they enable the widespread belief in a hopeful, eschatological trajectory for law, politics, and human existence. In short, "values" are the secular equivalent of God—they are the continuation of theology by other means.

What then is the ontological status of these divinities in any given context? It is important to answer this question because the ontological status of these divinities will affect what one thinks of them and what can be done with them. It is important to be able to discern in any given context to what extent values are *ontologically deep* and to what extent they are *ontologically superficial.* Values are ontologically deep to the extent that they constitute the dominant forms of being of an individual or a group. Conversely, values are ontologically superficial to the extent that they are relegated to subordinate or derivative forms of being of an individual or a group.[10] If in a given context, values and value-talk are ontologically superficial—for instance, if they are a kind of epiphenomenal, normatively pleasing illusion akin to magical thinking—then participating in value-talk on its own terms is probably not intellectually interesting. If, by contrast, in a given context, values are ontologically deep—for instance, if they are sedimented cultural formations that constitute the very way in which our social and intellectual lives are fashioned—then engaging in value-talk might well be not only intellectually interesting, but even morally or politically important.

The identification of the ontological status of values in any given instance will help fashion an appropriate orientation toward the invocation of "values": committed participation, pious reverence, sustained skepticism, intellectual disengagement, strategic use, or still some other orientation. Now, making determinations about the ontological depth or superficiality of values may seem complicated (and very often it is), presenting difficult questions of philosophy, social theory, and aesthetics. Instead of dealing with these difficult questions, consider first as an easy, illustrative case the difference between the ontology of values in Sophocles' *Antigone* and the ontology of values in a Mobil Oil advertisement.

In Sophocles' play, the value of loyalty to family so pervades the being of Antigone that she deliberately brings disaster not only upon herself, but upon her father and upon the state. We do not doubt the depth of Antigone's valuation of loyalty to family precisely because we see the extreme pain that she is willing to create in vindicating this loyalty to family. By contrast, the pro-

fessed commitment to values contained in Mobil ads is designed
to achieve strategic advantages largely (if not entirely) unrelated
to the observance or realization of those professed values.[11] We
understand this point implicitly—indeed, without effort—because we understand implicitly the character of corporate advertising. What gives the Mobil ad away is not some flaw in the
moral "substance" of its arrangement of normatively pleasing
"value" signs, but rather in the recognition that Mobil is an oil
company and that its text occupies the aesthetic space of a corporate advertisement. Few of us are likely to confuse the ontological
status of Antigone's values with those of a Mobil Oil ad.

But this is an easy case. It has been framed that way—precisely
to illustrate a difference between values that are ontologically
deep and values that are ontologically superficial. Although the
case, as framed here, is easy, applying the distinction remains
problematic. In other contexts, such as law review articles or legal
scholarship generally, the ontological status of values and value-
talk is more controversial.

For instance, many American legal thinkers still seem to believe (at some level) that the value-talk and the normative prescriptions of their legal scholarship have some significant *normative effect* on the decisions of courts or other official actors. As I
have argued elsewhere, however, this a priori belief in the normative efficacy of value-talk is a kind of *deformation professionelle.*
Indeed, the *normative effect* of value-talk in American legal
thought does not go much farther than organizing the arrangement of normatively pleasing signs in a way that fashions normatively self-flattering modes of self-presentation for its authors and
readers. In short, *the normative effect* of value-talk in the academy
does not go much further than sustaining a mode of discourse
that enables those who transact in "law" to do so while represent-
ing themselves as engaged in a morally or politically admirable
enterprise. In turn, this professional self-representation does not
have much more ontological depth than the self-representations
of Mobil Oil in its advertisements.

It would be useful, then, to begin understanding value-talk in American legal thought as a mode of advertising—advertising for the institutions, devices, and techniques of "law." One would then understand that "values" are related to these institutions, devices, and techniques of law in the same ambiguous ways as in any other kind of commercial advertising. From this perspective, the project of participating in legal thought to advance moral or political "values" would be on the same order (and just as promising) as trying to advance moral or political values by securing employment with an advertising firm. In short, it would be a category mistake—a particularly profound category mistake.

From the perspective of value-talk, these points are, of course, very difficult to grasp. In part, that is because value-talk presupposes its own ontological depth. And ironically, it is precisely because value-talk presupposes its own ontological depth that it can easily become an ontologically superficial enterprise—one where values are professed, refined, exchanged, ranked, reconceptualized, and recycled in a carnival of PR images. This is, of course, precisely what the Mobil ad illustrates: the appropriation of moral and political value signs for ends of self-promotion.

The Performative Roles of Values

Closely associated with the ontological status of values and value-talk is a question about their performative roles. It is one thing to deal with values as rigorously defined *concepts*—the sort of brittle artifacts one encounters in the most arid analytical philosophy. It is another thing to deal with values as *totems* of social institutions. And it is still another thing to deal with values as *motivational orientations* in guilt and shame complexes.

To say that values can be concepts, motivational orientations, or totems is to recognize that, in any given context, "values," or any given "value," can have a different ontological status. And, of course, "values" do not in and of themselves reveal their own ontological status. The value sign "justice," for instance, can play the role of concept, image, ideal, motivation, totem, icon, affect, coercive device (and so on).

Precisely because "justice" may have a different ontological status in different contexts, its performative roles might well differ. It might be, for instance, that the concept "justice" is used to persuade or justify, that the totem "justice" is used to identify or organize a political grouping, and that the motivational orientation "justice" is used to shame certain parties into performing or not performing certain actions. But it would be a serious mistake to conflate or confuse the various performative roles played by "justice," the concept, "justice," the totem, and "justice," the motivational orientation. And indeed, there is no particular reason to believe that justice as a concept means or is organized or operates in exactly the same way as "justice" as a motivational affective orientation or in the same way as "justice" as a totem. There is no reason to suppose transitivity among these ontological modal forms. Thus, it remains a question what relations hold among "justice" as a concept, "justice" as a totem, and "justice" as motivational orientation.

It is important to ask these questions about the performative role of values and value-talk because the identity of their roles cannot be determined a priori. And merely because values as artifacts are constituted as context-transcending, regulative grounds does not mean that they necessarily or usually or even often play those roles. Indeed, there is no a priori reason to believe that representations (say, fairness or God) govern in a self-determining way the practices in which their names are regularly invoked (court proceedings or holy war, respectively).

Like God, values feature in many roles. Values can serve as mediations in conversations. Values can also be media for the advancement of interests unrelated to the moral, political, or aesthetic charge of the values. They can be a form of compensation for and escapism from a degraded reality.[12] Values and value-talk can operate as a form of collective denial, a way of not taking into account the social or historical situation.[13] Values and value-talk can operate as vehicles of coercion, guilt, or shame. Values and value-talk can be a way of arresting troubling and disturbing inquiries. And in turn, all of these performative roles can, depending on the situation and the perspective, themselves be (however problematic such a determination might be) morally appealing, morally unappealing, or some combination of the two.

Viewed from the perspective of value-talk, values are typically seen as extremely valuable. They tend to play very good roles. I do not want to dispute that values can indeed play those roles some of the time. But the characteristic presupposition of value-talk (both in analytical moral philosophy and American jurisprudence) is that these valued roles are somehow fundamental, primary, or essential to values—while the less seemly uses of value-talk are a kind of "abuse." [14] This kind of aesthetic frame— this normatively loaded aesthetic frame—is not a prerequisite for thinking about values or how they are used. It is, however, a prerequisite for engaging in value-talk.

In and of itself, there is nothing wrong with this sort of disciplinary freeze-framing of identities; nothing wrong, of course, so long as we remember not to equate the world established in value-talk with our own. Before we do make such an equation, it would be necessary to ask the ontological and the performative questions.

Value Section 2.1

In order to ascertain the ontological status and the performative role of "values" in any given context, it is necessary to examine the relations between values on the one hand, and the practices and discourses in which they are invoked on the other. [15] Now, of course, to the extent that one begins from a position committed to the sanctity of values as values, this examination will not go too far. The point is obvious: one cannot inquire into the ontological status or the performative role of God simply by asking him (or his representatives) think about the matter.

It is important to ask these questions about the ontological
status and the performative role of values. As an example, consider some prescriptions from the recent MacCrate Report, *The
Statement of Fundamental Lawyering Skills and Professional Values
of the ABA Task Force on Law Schools and the Profession:*

> **Value Section 2: Striving to Promote Justice, Fairness,
> and Morality. As a member of a profession that bears
> special responsibility for the quality of justice, a lawyer
> should be committed to the values of:**
> **2.1 Promoting Justice, Fairness and Morality in One's
> Own Daily Practice** [16]

In one sense, this section seems really quite moral. It has lots of
moral value signs packed in, and they all sound good. But
bracket, for one moment, the normative allure of section 2.1 and
consider a matter of aesthetics. Consider for one moment the
mediations deployed between "lawyers" on the one hand, and
"justice," "fairness," and "morality" on the other. Notice that
according to section 2.1, a lawyer need not actually do anything
to promote justice, fairness, or morality. He or she need only be
committed. What is more, the lawyer need not be committed to
justice, fairness, or morality. He or she need only be committed
to the *values* of promoting justice, etc. Finally, he or she need not
be committed to the values of justice, fairness, or morality in
themselves, but must only be committed to the values of *promoting* justice, fairness, and morality.

When we get to the ABA's actual discussion of this section, we
find not only discussion, but further limitations on this commitment to promoting certain selected values. I am referring specifically to subsections 2.1(a), 2.1(b), and 2.1(c), which read as
follows:

> **As a member of a profession that bears special respon-
> sibilities for the quality of justice [citations omitted], a
> lawyer should be committed to the values of:**

2.1. Promoting Justice, Fairness and Morality in One's Own Daily Practice, including:

(a) To the extent required or permitted by the ethical rules of the profession, acting in conformance with considerations of justice, fairness and morality when making decisions or acting on behalf of a client (see Skill Section 6.1(a)(iii)(B) *supra*);

(b) To the extent required or permitted by the ethical rules of the profession, counseling clients to take considerations of justice, fairness and morality into account when the client makes decisions or engages in conduct that may have an adverse effect on other individuals or on society (see Skill Section 6.1(a)(i-ii)(A) *supra*);

(c) Treating other people (including clients, other attorneys, and support personnel) with dignity and respect.[17]

While it is tempting to explore further this excruciatingly objectivist representation of values, such an exercise is not necessary. It is not necessary because the ontological superficiality of this representation of values is obvious. Indeed, in the context of actual legal practice—a practice that is almost always success oriented, invariably strategic, and relentlessly coercive—it does not seem that this recommendation is likely to accomplish very much in the way of actually promoting justice, morality, or fairness. So what are these values doing here? And why recommend these values?

Here they are—subsectioned, limited by exceptions and cross-references, sliced and diced, cut and pasted—a complex schedule of objectivist labels and formulas reminiscent of a statutory code. Of course, one could give a traditional normative argument criticizing this particular kind of value-talk, presenting normative reasons why this form of objectivist representation of values is ethically or morally deficient. But that would miss the point. The point is not to render a moral or ethical judgment on our ways of talking about values, but rather to achieve an appreciation of the aesthetic inadequacy of the way in which this talk of "values" is conducted. The point is not to formulate a "reason," an "objection," or an "argument," but *to develop an aesthetic capacity, an intellectual competence, a quality of mind, to appreciate the utterly degraded form of life exemplified in the MacCrate report's re-presentation of values.*

We have returned to the observation with which this essay began: values are constituted by being severed from their generative history. In section 2.1, "values" are a technocratic aggregation of feel-good signs linked together in a happy-talk jurisprudence that is almost completely removed from any act of valuation or any generative history. Having been stripped of any generative history, these "values" in section 2.1 mean virtually nothing at all. They are simply the simulation of moral concern or ethical commitment.

Once emancipated from their generative history, values tend to become the ethical equivalent of currency—endlessly recyclable, ready for appropriation by any force, ready to underwrite any end. The identities of values become uncertain, their roles indiscriminate. But this is . . .

POETIC JUSTICE

And it should not surprise. What else is to be expected of an enterprise that seeks to sever itself from its own history and forget that history? Value-talk, as it is practiced in so much analytical moral philosophy and American jurisprudence, is very much that project. Now that values have become radically emancipated from their generative history, it surely cannot surprise that values should be ontologically insecure, prone to identity crises and indiscriminate use.

Some thinkers apparently believe that we must shrink from such realizations, for they put our whole normative universe and our political projects in question. But it is only a frightened or weary perspective that confuses putting something at risk—life, values, anything—with its devaluation.[18] That frightened and weary perspective—call it "nihilism" or, at this point, call it "law"—is the one that knows how to question its gods, its values, but dares not do so for fear of confronting a loss that it knows, on some level, has already occurred.

FOUR

The Evaluation Controversy

During the early 1990s, a number legal academics became concerned with the "evaluation" of legal scholarship. Some of the concern was precipitated by the emergence of new genres of legal scholarship — the "narrative scholarship" practiced by critical race theory thinkers, and the interdisciplinary and transdisciplinary (not to mention, the anti-disciplinary) work that also emerged at that time.

The legal academy thus experienced a kind of belated anxiety over the legal canon. A number of essays were written about how to evaluate the emerging genres. A small cottage industry developed discussing how to evaluate legal scholarship — particularly the new genres.

Interestingly, it seems not to have occurred to anyone that after a hundred years of academic doctrinal exegesis the main evaluation problem might well lie not so much with the emerging genres, but rather with the traditional ones. Specifically, one might have asked: How is one to evaluate examples of the traditional doctrinal genre when all its rhetorical moves have already been made — in fact, many times over? What sort of scholarly achievement or quality of mind is sought in such kinds of traditional scholarship? What can fairly be asked of this kind of scholarship? In what sense is it scholarship at all? And why do it?

By and large, such questions were not asked. Instead, the focus on how to evaluate the new genres of scholarship served to elide such questions. The receipt of the new genres within the framework of evaluation served as a precritical reaffirmation of the value of the traditional genres. It was, in effect, a reassertion of the primacy of legalist aesthetics and jural form within legal scholarship itself. The felt need to define proper evaluation standards or criteria was an expression of the juridical impulse—the desire to say (like judges) what the law is. It was a way of reaffirming the possibility of meaningful law-like norms—of rule-like or standard-like criteria.

In law, the evaluation question is, in its very form, a kind of distraction. To the usual questions ("Should the legal canon be expanded?" "Is the legal canon still serving present needs?" Should the legal canon be supplemented?") one would need to take a more forthright, a more incredulous, attitude. One would need to ask the more fundamental question: "What legal canon?" as in "What are you talking about?"

It is toward the presentation of this question that the following essay aims. What is involved in "presentation" of the question here is more than simply putting the question into words. (That has already been done.) What is involved is a disclosure of an already existing need to ask this *question—a disclosure of how the question arises, why it must be answered, and why it won't go away.*

The essay, which was originally entitled "Pre-figuration and Evaluation," was written as a response to one of the most intellectually perspicuous efforts to deal with the evaluation question: Ed Rubin's "On Beyond Truth: A Theory for Evaluating Legal Scholarship."

Evaluation is hard to do. It is particularly hard to do once the cultural and conceptual reifications that establish the boundedness, location, and identity of "author," "text," and "reader" have become unhinged. With these crucial ontological determinants in question, it becomes difficult to separate what one projects into, or out of, the texts of others from what the authors invest in the texts themselves. If you are not convinced, consider the following sample evaluations.

This is what Gadamer says of Habermas:

> The concept of reflection and bringing to awareness that Habermas employs (admittedly from his sociological interest) appears to me, then, to be itself encumbered with dogmatism, and indeed, to be a misinterpretation of reflection.[1]

This is what Habermas says of Foucault:

> Foucault cannot adequately deal with the persistent problems that come up in connection with an interpretive approach to the object domain, a self-referential denial of universal validity claims, and a normative justification for critique.[2]

This is what Foucault says of Derrida:

> [O]bscurantisme terroriste.[3]

This is what Derrida says of Gadamer:

> Does not this way of speaking, in its very necessity, belong to a particular epoch, namely, that of a metaphysics of the will?[4]

These statements evince significant intellectual disagreement. How are we to evaluate these evaluations? Does this "situation" present a problem? Maybe. It depends on how this "situation" has been pre-figured. For Jean-François Lyotard, the French postmodern philosopher, this "situation" might be understood as an instantiation of a very serious problem, whereas for Hans-Georg Gadamer, the German Heideggerian, it would likely not.

For Lyotard, the "situation" here could be likened to a "differend." According to Lyotard, a differend arises when the regulation of a conflict is done in the idiom of one of the parties — an idiom in which the claims and arguments of the other party cannot be expressed and thus do not register.[5] For Lyotard, our institutionalized idioms, our verification procedures, our mechanisms for adjudicating truth, are preestablishing the realities whose truth we then assert.[6] If this is the kind of pre-figuration at work in the evaluation of scholarship, then our "situation" is a serious intellectual and political problem.

While Lyotard describes a highly problematic kind of *pre-figuration*, Gadamer's take is far more congenial to the confident self-image of conventional legal thought. For Gadamer, the recognition that we interpret texts through our own anticipated meanings and forestructures of understanding is not a problem at all. Rather, understanding is a process of revising one's preconceptions as one proceeds in the reading.[7] The structure of understanding is thus circular. This hermeneutic circle is not something to complain about; it is rather an ontological aspect of understanding itself.[8]

If we were to think of evaluation in terms of Lyotard's "differend," we would get a different vision of evaluation than if we thought about it in terms of Gadamer's "hermeneutic circle." For Lyotard, the appropriate response is

[t]o give the differend its due[, that] is to institute new addressees, new addressors, new significations and new referents. . . . What is at stake in a literature, in a philosophy, in a politics perhaps, is to bear witness to differends by finding idioms for them.[9]

For Gadamer the appropriate response is

> to be aware of one's own bias, so that the text may present
> itself in all its newness and thus be able to assert its own
> truth against one's own fore-meanings. . . . It is not, then, at
> all a case of safeguarding ourselves against the tradition that
> speaks out of the text but, on the contrary, to keep every-
> thing away that could hinder us in understanding it in terms
> of the thing.[10]

The important point to recognize here is that the divergent
responses of Lyotard and Gadamer have already been pre-scripted
in their divergent aesthetic pre-figurations. To generalize the
point: *normative prescription is largely already a matter of aesthetic
pre-figuration.*[11]

What to do? Is the question here who should we *choose* to help
us think about evaluation—Gadamer or Lyotard or someone
else? Maybe. But then again, framing the question in terms of a
"choice" is itself another idiomatic *pre-figuration*, one that is so
conventional in American legal thought that we can barely notice
that in speaking of "choice," something rather contestable has
been authorized, something which, in all its self-evident simplic-
ity often denies the significance of *pre-figuration.*[12]

It would seem, then, that there is no getting away from *pre-
figuration.* Pre-figuration is already reflexively happening everywhere. Habermas,[13] Gadamer,[14] Foucault,[15] Derrida,[16] and Lyotard[17]—different as their pre-figurations and their accounts of
pre-figuration may be—would each in his own way agree.

Once one recognizes this relentless logic of pre-figuration, it
becomes interesting to consider just how theories of evaluation or
evaluative criteria can forestall the kind of bias, prejudice, and
abuse of power in scholarly evaluation. Indeed, just how will
the evaluative criteria, the theory of evaluation, escape the pre-
figurations that lead to bias, prejudice, and abuse of power?
Rubin argues that "a theory of evaluation that provides alternative

criteria for defining boundaries and regulating debate can serve as a means of *controlling* ideological bias."[18]

The question is, how?

Within the conventional pre-figurations of contemporary legal thought, the answer is obvious: as Rubin argues, "[a]n articulated, coherent theory of evaluation provides a means of *disciplining* these reactions."[19] Now, to many people this claim will seem simply just true—in the manner that one's own pre-figurations always seem simply just true. But the questions remain: How will evaluative criteria discipline biased reactions? How will these evaluative criteria escape the partisan contaminations of those who do the evaluating?

The answer again is in the pre-figuration. Rubin, true to conventional contemporary legal academic form, pre-figures his evaluative criteria as *separate* and *distinct* from those who do the evaluating (you, me, etc.). This is the logic of objectivism reemerging on the level of form, of aesthetics. The evaluative criteria gain their integrity—they acquire their immunity from partisan contamination—by virtue of their separate and distinct existence.

But how has this separation been effectuated? Rubin writes: "These criteria, *interposed between* the reader and the text, *create the distance* necessary to evaluate a familiar work in some conscious and coherent fashion."[20] Here there is a conventional metaphor at work—one so commonplace in legal thought that we might not even recognize the metaphor or the aesthetic it enacts. And yet it is this spatial arrangement of reader/criteria/text that creates the *distance* and the boundaries *between* the evaluative criteria and those who do the evaluating.[21] And it is through the creation of these separate bounded domains that the evaluative criteria gain their apparent integrity and their apparent conceptual security from the partisan contaminations of the evaluators.

Now, as helpful as this spatial aesthetic appears to be in securing the integrity and conceptual security of evaluative criteria from the actions of evaluators, it nonetheless presents a signal difficulty for anyone who wants to adopt it as his or her own. The difficulty is that this spatial aesthetic is inert. If evaluative criteria are somehow to "control" ideology or to "discipline" bi-ased reactions (in other words, to perform some action), then some additional moving imagery must be introduced to motivate or create this "controlling" or "disciplining" action.

In Rubin's analysis, as in much of conventional legal thought itself, this moving imagery is provided by an instrumentalist frame—the calculus of means and ends. And indeed, Rubin repeatedly describes his evaluative criteria as means designed to promote the end of sound evaluation. In his own words, a coher-ent theory of evaluation provides "*a means* of disciplining"[22] evaluative reactions; "*the means* by which a discipline reassesses its own evaluative criteria";[23] and "*a means* of controlling ideological bias."[24]

So we have *means* (evaluative criteria) and we have *ends* (sound evaluations) and together these means and ends are supposed to regulate evaluation of scholarship. But notice that even with this instrumentalist frame to structure the action we still need something more to motivate, to animate the action. What is missing? Answer: A subject, an agent—the evaluator. But the evaluator is not here. Where is he?

Rubin does not write very much about this subject, this agent, this evaluator. The reason is simple: this subject, this agent, this evaluator is something of an intellectual embarrassment. It is he, after all, who is supposed to be "disciplined" and "controlled" by means of the evaluative criteria. And yet now it turns out that it is precisely through him, through his pre-figurations, that the *means* and the *ends* of evaluation discussed by Rubin will acquire their actual significance and meaning. It is his pre-figurations that make the evaluative criteria mean something in the first place.

In both the figure of the evaluator as well as in Rubin's pre-figuration of the problem of evaluation, there is an important tension. *It is a tension that remains unresolved throughout conventional legal thought.* Here it is emerging in full form:

> Ideology has the interesting attribute of making opposing normative beliefs seem incorrect—not as a matter of normative debate, but as a matter of objective truth. The comprehensive quality of ideology, moreover, means that those who subscribe to it do not perceive it as an ideology at all, but simply as the proper way to view the world. . . . A theory of evaluation that provides alternative criteria for defining boundaries and regulating debate can serve as a means of controlling ideological bias.[25]

No sooner does Rubin affirm, quite appropriately, the invisibility of ideology to those who are within its grip than he sets this insight aside to claim that a theory of evaluation can provide "alternative criteria . . . as a means of controlling ideological bias."[26] The question is, how? How can evaluative prescription, in and of itself, modify aesthetic pre-figuration if the former is always already shaped and understood through the latter? This is a question that conventional legal thought does not ask. It simply presumes, it simply pre-figures the answer. *The effectiveness of evaluative prescription is simply assumed (as in law itself) to be ontologically adequate to regulate its objects.*

Once one recognizes the importance of pre-figuration to evaluation, the integrity, conceptual security, and transcendence that conventional legal thought typically accords to evaluative prescription dissolve. Evaluative prescription is just as susceptible to the practice of bias, intolerance, authoritarianism—even cruelty, if you want—as any other kind of human discourse. Prescription, normative discourse, and evaluative criteria are not self-determining; they do not, indeed cannot, rest on their own bottom. They can be used to do anything—anything at all so long as it is enabled by the aesthetic, rhetorical, and social pre-figurations of those involved.

This means (among other things) that the ritualized and pro-
fessionalized *advocacy* of virtue so characteristic of conventional
legal thought does not necessarily, or even presumptively, coincide with or advance the *practice* of virtue.

Now my guess is that for many legal academics—particularly
those most enthralled by the formulation, justification, and evaluation of normative prescriptions—this is not an entirely welcome
realization. It is destabilizing and disorienting. But do not let this
distract. It's happening.

In Rubin's article, as in conventional legal thought itself, the logic
of pre-figuration is represented as subordinate to the logic of
normative prescription. But as we have just seen, this subordination of pre-figuration to evaluation is itself an ironic aesthetic
entailment of the conventional pre-figurations deployed in Rubin's article. The irony then is that the recurrent subordination of
the aesthetic to the normative in conventional legal thought is
effectuated on the plane of the aesthetic itself—an aesthetic
which, conventional legal thought must, for its own well-being,
routinely fail to notice.

To generalize the point: one might say that the whole focus on
"evaluation" in contemporary debates about legal thought is itself
a conventional pre-figuration—one that disables recognition of
the problematic state of conventional legal thought. Indeed,
"evaluation" is the conventional way of simultaneously taking
cognizance and avoiding recognition of a much more sweeping,
much more significant problem—namely, the ongoing breakdown of conventional legal thought and the systemic denial of
this breakdown.

"Evaluation" is the delimited conceptual site where professional
academic anxieties over loss of standards, loss of meaning, loss of
power are expressed, registered, and ultimately defused in a ritualized reenactment of standard-form legal arguments about
merit, standards, bias, and so on. Framing the problem as one of

evaluation and lack of evaluative criteria pre-figures it in such a way that the problem already appears amenable to resolution with ordinary juridical means (a *better* theory, *new* criteria, *clearer* standards). This enables a performative confirmation that the dominant paradigm and its conceptual moves are still capable of doing work, still capable of providing solutions after all these years. Indeed, if the problem is one of evaluation, we, as legal thinkers, will have no problems transposing all the arguments, the rhetoric we have developed in our writings on the closely related subject of adjudication.

Similarly, the focus of attention on "theories," "methods," and "criteria" enables a comforting location of the problem, its analysis, and its resolution in a safe place—in stabilized object-forms ostensibly external to legal thinkers. We are thus reprieved from recognizing that the problems of bias, prejudice, and abuse of power lie closer to home—in *us,* in *our pre-figurations.* Perhaps more important, this reprieves us from recognizing that the conventional jurisprudential and political matrices that make our positions, our stances, our normative projects at once intelligible and meaningful are unraveling, are decomposing.

But what is it that is unraveling, that is decomposing? It is what is generally considered to be the sum total of American legal scholarship. It is precisely the enterprise that is considered virtually exhaustive of legal scholarship. Again Rubin provides a good description:

> Legal scholarship generally consists of normative statements about the way that government decisions should be made. These statements can be understood as prescriptions addressed to the relevant decisionmaker: most frequently a judge, but also a legislator or administrator. The scholar may not literally be addressing the decisionmaker. . . . The notion of a prescription addressed to a particular decisionmaker describes the conceptual structure of the work, the way in which its arguments are formulated.[27]

Now, what Rubin describes here as a kind of thought, a genre of scholarship, I describe more broadly as a social and rhetorical practice, as "normative legal thought,"[28] as the contemporary form of the "Langdellian paradigm."[29] Normative legal thought establishes the appropriate roles, activities, rhetorics, aesthetics, personas, and concerns of legal academics. This practice is so well internalized that until recently it was not noticed,[30] much less questioned.[31] Normative legal thought was simply what one did.

But now that this practice is decomposing, we notice it. We even notice how it is decomposing. It is decomposing in the manner in which social practices usually decompose — the participants can no longer sustain the beliefs, or suspensions of disbelief, necessary to make the practice meaningful to them or to others.[32]

Indeed, Rubin's own description of this sort of thought *itself* already reflects the signs of disenchantment and demoralization. Consider one of Rubin's statements above: "The scholar may not *literally* be addressing the decisionmaker."[33] But why not *literally?* The answer is obvious: there is no apparent instrumental or intrinsic value in doing so. By and large, neither judges nor any other bureaucratic decision makers are listening to academic advice that they are not already prepared to believe. There is thus very little instrumental value in addressing judges or any other bureaucratic decision makers. As for the intrinsic value of addressing judges, it is rather weak. To write to judges entails the adoption of their idioms, their aesthetic, their rhetoric — in short, their discursive practices. Are the discursive practices of these bureaucratic state agents somehow intellectually edifying? Morally enlightening? Aesthetically enlivening? Doubtful.

And thus it is no surprise that many legal academics have already abandoned "*literally* . . . addressing the decision maker." Instead, they address their own idealized decision maker — their own Hercules, their own version of Dworkin's mythical appellate judge. This is, however, a weak and transitional practice. It strives to retain for itself the sense of power and authority made possible by the conventional paradigm at its zenith, while at the same time trying to enact a discourse of some intellectual integrity. But ironically, in trying to achieve both, it achieves neither. It pretends to an authority and a power that it self-evidently lacks, while at the same time foreclosing itself from pursuing more interesting intellectual possibilities.

What is more, this transitional practice provides only a false and momentary security, for it is the kind of self-deception that already knows itself to be a self-deception. Why write to an imaginary or idealized judge when it is obvious that imaginary or idealized judges can be whatever one wants them to be? Rubin writes: "The notion of a prescription addressed to a particular decisionmaker describes the conceptual structure of the work, the way in which its arguments are formulated."[34] Exactly so. But why would one want to engage in such a practice? How could it be meaningful to argue within constraints one already knows to be a projection of false necessity?[35] One can understand why law students do moot court. Law students are on their way to becoming lawyers. They are learning rhetorical skills. How do we explain, however, fully grown legal academics playing moot court? How do they explain this to themselves?

One may talk in false and ugly idioms when justified by sound instrumental reasons (some kinds of litigation, for example). One may also talk in instrumentally ineffectual idioms when the practice of the talk is its own end (some kinds of philosophy, for example). But when the idiom is false and ugly, and when it secures no valued instrumental goal at all, it is difficult to see why anyone would engage in it at all.

That is precisely our situation—the situation of normative legal thought. The surfacing of these questions has left the practice of normative legal thought increasingly demoralized and disenchanted. The questions do not go away. They multiply. Indeed, a multitude of new questions are now surfacing that make the practice of normative legal thought appear increasingly artificial—a kind of flimsy, ineffectual, and often quite self-righteous posturing. Consider just two such questions.

First, why should legal thinkers unreflectively identify (at any level of abstraction) with an actual or idealized *state agent*—the judge? There seems to be no sound political or moral reason why legal thinkers should *a priori* adopt and identify with the concerns, idioms, and power perspectives of judges or any other "public" decision makers. Such an unreflective self-identification seems particularly unwarranted and unjustified after the conceptual and material collapse of the public and private spheres and the accompanying politicization of the agencies of the state, including the judiciary. Indeed, the self-identification of the legal thinker with the actual or idealized judge yields a professional rhetoric that legitimizes the courts, the legal profession, and the positive law. In reinterpreting legal materials "to make them the best they can be,"[36] legal thinkers in effect serve as a kind of P.R. firm for the bureaucratic state. Why would intellectuals unreflectively enlist their minds to support such an unspecified, and potentially objectionable, enterprise?

Second, why should academics adopt the intellectual perspectives of actual or idealized judges and legislators? Such borrowing commits the legal academic to running well-traveled analytical mazes through archaic metaphysical conceptions of intent, causation, choice, free will, authorship, and the rational self, to name a few. To adopt the perspectives, stances, idioms, conceptual schemes, and social aesthetics of actual or idealized judges yields a highly impoverished intellectual universe. Again the questions for the legal thinker are: Why would one do this? How could it be meaningful?

For legal thinkers of past generations, these questions did not and could not arise. They could not arise because those legal thinkers were so successfully self-identified with a projected image of the actual or idealized appellate judge.[37] Indeed, for those legal thinkers, this epic self-identification was constitutive of their very being, their very activities as legal thinkers.

But today, this role conflation is revealed to be role confusion, and with this revelation, the legal thinker's sense of his own intellectual significance and worldly power dissipates. The figure of the appellate judge—much as legal thinkers may romanticize him (think: Hercules)—is nonetheless not a cultural nor an intellectual giant. On the contrary, this is someone whose vision and understanding of actual cases and controversies is sharply delimited and highly stylized. This is someone whose access to the "facts" of the case is mediated by two or more professional actors whose very raison d'être is to coax, manipulate, and coerce the court into reaching a predetermined outcome. This is someone invested with significant power to make very difficult decisions that entail serious consequences on the basis of very little information under extreme time pressure. This is the figure of authority: the one authorized to close the dialogue with a very monological *ipse dixit.* Let us not deceive ourselves. This is not the sort of persona likely to produce a particularly open, searching, or intellectually curious rhetorical practice. Not at all: "Judges are people of violence. Because of the violence they command, judges characteristically do not create law, but kill it. Theirs is the jurispathic office. Confronting the luxuriant growth of a hundred legal traditions, they assert that *this one* is law and destroy or try to destroy the rest."[38] Not surprisingly, those legal thinkers with the most serious intellectual inclinations try to take distance from this core persona.

But given the pervasiveness of the core image throughout jurisprudence, legal rhetoric, and even the professional self, "taking distance" turns out to be difficult. True, legal thinkers often claim to "take distance" from the conscious identification with the figure of the appellate judge. But such conscious stance-taking typically leaves the pre-figured unconscious self-identification with the appellate judge unnoticed, undisturbed, and unreconstructed—still shaping jurisprudence, legal thought, and the professional self. The result is that philosophy, social science, literary criticism, economics, and linguistics are transformed (and denatured) into a set of pat authorities—footnote material for the legal thinker's brief in support of her "positions" or his "stances."[39]

Indeed, there is nothing at all—no body of knowledge, no learning, no insight, no emotion, no critique—that the legal academic will not transform (and denature) into a source of prescription, into a regulatory device, into a norm, into more grist for the normative legal-thought mill.

The simultaneous decomposition of normative legal thought along with its continued hold on our jurisprudential imaginations yields two seemingly contradictory, yet reciprocally parasitic tendencies. The first, which has already been described, is a kind of flattening out, a homogenization of our thought. The second is an accelerating proliferation of difference, differentiation, and pluralism.

The more legal thought embraces difference, differentiation, and plurality, the more it stays the same. The celebration of difference and the embrace of plurality are neutralized by the homogenizing rhetoric of normative legal thought—a rhetoric that the champions of difference, differentiation, and plurality (various self-identified pragmatists, contextualists, postmodernists, feminists, and others) self-defeatingly believe they have already overcome.

This gruesome homogenization, this implosion of intellectual possibility, this flattening of the jurisprudential universe, in turn, prompts an excited and sometimes desperate search for something else, for some intellectual perspective that will provide some "purchase on," or some "escape from," our "situation." It is thus in the conscious or unconscious responses to the decomposition of normative legal thought that the fragmentation of legal thought proliferates.

All of these forces—the self-identification of the legal thinker with the appellate judge and the unraveling of this self-identification; the homogenizing rhetoric of normative legal thought and the proliferation of difference in legal thought; the decomposition of normative legal thought and the denial of this decomposition—produce bias, prejudice, and abuse of power in the evaluation of legal thought.

The self-identification of the legal thinker with the projected image of the actual or idealized appellate judge yields a kind of authoritarian pre-figuration of evaluation. It establishes the evaluator's idiom, rhetoric, and knowledge base as a court of reason—entitled to rule and beyond challenge, except in the most narrow, already prescripted ways. The unraveling of this self-identification, on the other hand, leaves the evaluator without a stable sense of professional identity. The evaluator is thus left without anything other than the self's unrationalized preferences as an evaluative frame.

The homogenizing rhetoric of normative legal thought leads to a flattened intellectual universe—the night in which all cows are black.[40] The proliferation of difference, on the other hand, makes it difficult for any legal thinker to understand why any other legal thinker would be asking the kinds of questions he is, presumably, trying to answer.

The decomposition of normative legal thought means that there is no sound shared understanding for making evaluative decisions. The denial of this decomposition means that this decomposing paradigm nonetheless continues to reproduce itself unconsciously through its evaluative criteria and its evaluative decisions.

If this is an apt description of the present situation, then the sorts of abuses we experience or witness in the evaluation of legal scholarship—the under- or over-valorization of certain kinds of scholarship—are hardly going to be avoided by the prescription of evaluative criteria. Instead, this focus on evaluation will reprieve legal thinkers from recognizing a much more serious and pervasive problem—the unraveling of the conventional paradigm, the decomposition of normative legal thought.

In this respect, perhaps the most pervasive problem with the academic focus on "evaluation," on "maintaining standards" (and so on), is that it presumes, both in its substance and in its form, that the currently dominant practice of legal thought—namely, normative legal thought—has some redeeming social or intellectual value. This once-uncontroversial assumption is now very much in need of some serious intellectual demonstration.

III

MISSING SUBJECTS

FIVE

Contradiction and Denial

This essay started out as a book review of Mark Kelman's "A Guide to Critical Legal Studies" for the Michigan Law Review. Mark Kelman is one of the most acute thinkers of the "second generation" of critical legal studies thinkers. In 1988 he published his book on CLS. It was an impressive (and impressively comprehensive) tour of CLS writings to date.

Nonetheless, upon finishing the book, Kelman's approach seemed to me far too normatively oriented. Kelman was too interested in normative conclusions and too confident in the importance of the beliefs and arguments of legal academics. His views seemed far too rationalist in tenor—far too much of an effort to present CLS thought as some sort of conceptually coherent totalizing normative theory—the sort of disciplinary artifact that an analytical philosopher might take seriously (and worse, possibly, even like).

For me, however, the appeal of CLS thought was that, in its best moments, it eschewed this disciplinary drive to achieve theoretical totalization. The best of CLS thought was, in keeping with its own diagnosis of the situation, conflicted (not coherent), disclosive (not rationalist), and interstitial (not totalizing). At its best, CLS thought offered some powerful but nonetheless partial insights into the construction and organization of American law. If this assessment was right, then any attempt to present CLS thought as a coherent, ratio-nalist, grand normative theoretical totalization would, quite predict-ably, set it up for a fall.

This, among other things, is what I set out to write in the book review. But, it wouldn't write. Besides, rightly or wrongly, it did not seem to me appropriate at the time to write a critical review of critical legal studies thinkers. At the time, CLS thinkers were subject to all manner of adverse personnel action: nontenuring and nonhiring. They were also subject (as I learned later) to a great deal of less formal sanction within their own academic institutions.

The upshot was that I wrote one long book review rather critical of Kelman's book (and sent it to Michigan). I then wrote a second long book review still critical of Kelman's book (and sent it to Michigan). Both reviews were too critical and, as explained below, too creaky. I then wrote the following book unreview (and sent it to Michigan).

They politely, but very firmly, informed me it would be the final version. Here it is.

A GUIDE TO CRITICAL LEGAL STUDIES.
By *Mark Kelman.*
Cambridge: Harvard University Press. 1987. Pp. 360. $30.

I have now written several drafts of a review of Mark Kelman's *A Guide to Critical Legal Studies*—each draft more unwieldy, more cumbersome than the previous one.[1] In each draft, I found my-self, in good standard book review form, writing about (what Kelman writes about (what CLS scholars write about (what liberal legal thinkers write about (what they think they are doing (when they say they are doing (law)))))). Not only was it exceed-ingly difficult for me to keep the players and the plays straight, but I also had all sorts of difficulties keeping my subjects and direct objects in line.

Very quickly my subjects started trying to do some impossible (often barely mentionable) things to my direct objects. Whenever I allowed the term "CLS" or "liberal legal thought" to occupy the subject space of the sentence for even a moment, it would invariably try to slam-dance into the direct object, and I would invariably lose all linguistic control. After a few invocations, these linguistic subjects, "CLS" and "liberal legal thought," metamorphosed into metaphysical subjects, endowed with all the privileges appurtenant to that exalted status—privileges such as identity, constancy, integrity, unity, and many others that arguably each did not deserve. Soon these metaphysical subjects took over entirely and began trying to displace each other by making all the usual metaphysical moves.

And each time I finished a new draft, I ended up with yet another deeply caricatured description of CLS and liberal legal thought. Now, I have nothing against deep (or any other kind of) caricatures, but part of the purpose of caricatures is not simply to allow one to recognize the pattern, *but to recognize the pattern in the detail.* Somehow, where discussions of CLS are concerned, that last part seems to get lost, and very often CLS scholarship is reduced to some creaky abstraction like "contradiction/indeterminacy/legitimation."

This was happening in my drafts too. I kept trying to write about Kelman's major theme: the view that standard legal thought is characterized both by the presence of contradiction and the denial or repression of contradiction (pp. 2–3). I wanted to say two things about Kelman's double-edged theme. These two things were related (which was certainly a hopeful sign)—unfortunately, they were related paradoxically (which arguably was not).

The first thing: The reflexivity of legal thought is such that the question of whether standard legal thought denies or represses internal contradictions, as Kelman claims, is unlikely to yield an easy straightforward answer.

The second thing: Standard legal thought does in fact deny or repress contradiction in an easy, straightforward manner.

*   *   *

The longer version of these two things goes like this: Whether one agrees with Kelman's claim that standard legal thought represses its internal contradictions depends largely, I think, on the character of one's experience of law and legal thought. In turn, that experience, whether contradicted or coherent, depends very much on how one understands the self-image of law and legal thought. In turn, for people who are deeply implicated in the legal enterprise, the self-image of law and legal thought is in part a function of what they would like law and legal thought to be (and, of course, vice versa). All together, these observations about the reflexivity of law and legal thought caution that the question of whether standard legal thought denies or represses internal contradictions is unlikely to yield an easy, straightforward answer.[2]

Yet quite clearly, for standard legal thought, the answer is straightforward. Standard legal thought abhors contradiction. And it abhors paradox and incommensurability as well. In short, it abhors anything that it perceives as challenging its own self-image as an integrated, self-sufficient mode of thought that is naturally entitled to adjudicate and organize the character of social life. Indeed, despite widespread *substantive* agreement that legal thought is not an autonomous branch of knowledge,[3] *the form* of most contemporary legal thought indicates exactly the opposite.[4] Most legal thinkers continue to write and think as if legal thought were autonomous, even as they busily repudiate legal formalism (over and over again).

The continued entrapment of standard legal thought within the old forms of an autonomous body of knowledge is evidenced by the astonishing alacrity and the relentless systematicity with which it rejects anything (such as contradiction) that might challenge its own autonomy. Even two decades of sustained contact with foreign disciplines like economics, philosophy, and literature have failed to acquaint the legal mind with its lack of autonomy.

On the contrary, the foreign disciplines were immediately confined to the space of the "Law and ..." formula—where they were relegated to the subordinate role of supplying new content to replenish the structures of the old legal forms. As the expert witness is to the litigator, so apparently are the liberal arts to legal scholarship.

The almost complete subjugation of the foreign disciplines to the architectural needs of standard legal thought suggests that the legal mind is extraordinarily well equipped to overlook, deny, or repress even the most obvious and serious challenges to its own autonomy. And yet, in a paradoxical way (for it is only paradoxically that I can say this), the failure of standard legal thought to reckon seriously with these challenges is a failure of legal mind.[5] It is a failure of judgment, of self-awareness, of authenticity.[6] It is a failure of legal mind to take seriously its own reflexive character.

Indeed, or rather, paradoxically, standard legal thought offers a number of easy straightforward stratagems for the denial or repression of contradiction. Here are just a few.

Subject-Object Reversals. Many legal scholars understand CLS claims of contradiction as an assertion that an *object* (here law and legal thought) partakes of a certain *quality* (here contradiction). In other words, the claim is understood to be that contradiction is part of the nature of law and legal thought. Accordingly, if a legal thinker is interested in determining whether the claims of contradiction are correct or not, he or she must determine whether this object called law and legal thought really does exist, and whether it really is contradictory as claimed.

I expect that, for some people, this way of thinking about CLS claims of contradiction seems perfectly sensible—indeed, natural. It seems only natural to suppose that CLS claims of contradiction are about an object and that this object should have a nature or an identity—one that is independent of the observer's conception of that object. The major reason, however, that this way of thinking seems so natural is that it is pre-conscious projection. And yet, of course, once one makes these *pre-conscious projections* explicit (as I am doing now) they hardly seem natural at all. For instance, the paragraph immediately above *objectifies* law and legal thought, radically separates this objectified vision of law and legal thought from the subject (the legal thinker), and *externalizes* contradiction in the object (law and legal thought).

Of course, once one makes this pre-conscious projection explicit, it does not have much value as a denial stratagem. But if the radical separation, the objectification, and the externalization remain pre-conscious, we have a terrific denial technique. For one thing, the externalization of contradiction in an objectified vision of law and legal thought spares the legal thinker from any recognition that his or her own thought processes might themselves be contradicted. This, of course, leaves the legal thinker fully confident in his or her ability to adjudicate the coherence (or lack thereof) of the legal system from a place that is itself free from doubt.

One can see this process of projection at work in Dworkin's challenge to CLS claims of contradiction. Says Dworkin: "Nothing is easier or more pointless than demonstrating that a flawed and contradictory account fits as well as a smoother and more attractive one."[7] The argument seems to be that you too, like CLS scholars, can see contradiction everywhere, but why on earth would you want to? Now there is some bite to this claim. But the question is, what does it bite? If you ask me, it ends up biting its own tail.

But first, note that Dworkin is partly right in attacking the CLS method of contradictions: if one is trying to sort the debris of the world into theoretical categories, then choosing a contradictory categorization scheme (as opposed to a noncontradictory one) will facilitate the task greatly. Of course, Dworkin's objection can easily be turned against all sorts of traditional strategies for theory building—including some of his own. For instance, consider these variations:

1. Nothing is easier or more pointless than demonstrating that *an extremely abstract account* fits as well as a smoother and more attractive one.
2. Nothing is easier or more pointless than demonstrating that *an account that severely restricts or truncates the data to be interpreted* fits as well as a smoother and more attractive one.
3. Nothing is easier or more pointless than demonstrating that *an account that idealizes or sanitizes the hell out of the matters to be interpreted* fit as well as a smoother and more attractive one.

As these variations suggest, Dworkin's criticism has much broader possibilities than he imagines. In part, that is because the criticism is enabled not by any flaw in the targeted theory (CLS or any other) but by the implicit pre-conscious view of the targeted theory as a creation of a free subject radically separate from its object. If one is pre-consciously prepared to see a certain theory as having its origin in a subject radically separate from its object, then one will always be able to claim that constructing such a theory is "easy" in the pejorative Dworkinian sense. The problem, of course, is that it will be equally "easy" to make that claim. Things are just getting easier all the time.

Even the structure of the Subject-Object Reversal denial mechanism is simple. Consciously, we all know that subject and object are not radically separate. Pre-consciously, however, we often use metaphors that succeed nonetheless in radically separating the two (for example, inside/outside, here/there, etc.). When we project such crude and primitive views of subject-object relations onto the texts of others, we find (not surprisingly) that their texts are weak and flawed. The texts seem to contain views of subject-object relations that are simply untenable. Unfortunately, when we make this discovery, we are very often discovering something, not about the targeted theories, but about our own pre-conscious constructions.[8] Paradoxically, standard legal thought authorizes both the denial and the acknowledgment of this discovery. Denial is often easier. Acknowledgment is often more interesting. Both are sometimes appropriate.

Grand Solipsistic Theory. Standard legal theory seems increasingly strained in its rhetorical efforts to marginalize contradiction, paradox, and the like. One particularly popular denial strategy entails the development of a sort of "theoretical minimalism" where the criteria that theory sets up for the validation of law become so utterly unassuming in fact that, in an odd bow to Stanley Fish, these criteria are always already satisfied.[9] For instance, given a suitably specified universe, one gets the sense that virtually any state of affairs can be seen to conform with Kaldor-Hicks efficiency.[10] And try as one may, it still remains a mystery exactly what it is that is *really* ruled out by Dworkin's invitation to try to make of the legal materials the best they can be.[11]

What seems disquieting about the advent of these theories is not so much that they are wrong. Rather, it is the prospect that in their abstraction, emptiness, and utter lack of serious ambition for *the realization* of justice or other social virtues, these theories may well be an accurate expression of the current character of standard legal thought. Indeed, in the rush to resolve important normative matters, standard normative theory systematically and willingly subordinates normative positions to purely aesthetic criteria like coherence, consistency, and elegance. The result is that important social virtues (justice, equality) are subordinated to the aesthetics of the scholarly legal text. One might even begin to wonder what the social significance of this sort of scholarship really is: the promotion of justice and the social virtues, or the maintenance of rationalist form in legal thought?

The Really Good Judgment of American Pragmatism. In the valiant battle against the bureaucratization of law's empire, one cannot forget the great tradition of American pragmatism along with those wonderfully pithy sayings like: "think [. . .] not words,"[12] or "[t]he life of the law has not been [. . .]: it has been [. . .]."[13]

One problem with these bits of sensible advice is that they can seem downright quaint ... not a little oxymoronic, ... maybe even a little nonreferential too. Indeed, pragmatism has a great many things to recommend it, but one of them is not staying power. Indeed, even the contemporary proponents of pragmatism often seem not terribly pragmatic.

Pragmatism encourages us to make sense of our world not from the perspective of some philosophical idealism or rationalism, but in terms of intuitive judgments based on customs, traditions, and values embedded in the social context. This is great stuff, but it does pose some problems. One problem is that in our context it is precisely this sense that *there are* customs, traditions, and values embedded in the social context that is experienced as disappearing. Instead, we have the powerful rationalizing practices of bureaucracy and the market. So either the pragmatic invitation to look to context is a little vacant, or it is an invitation to surrender to whatever customs, traditions, and values the market and bureaucracy produce. My sense is that the invitation to pragmatism is both, and that the *current* conceptual vacancy of the pragmatic approach is precisely what allows bureaucracy and the market to determine its missing content and structure.

As if in confirmation, one often gets the sense that all the bold calls for a pragmatic renaissance in legal scholarship are just a glossy public relations cover for the promotion of the highly stylized rhetoric of the lawyer's brief. Adoption of such a rhetoric in legal scholarship leaves something to be desired. For one thing, it leaves legal academics without much to do other than cheer or hiss the courts from the sidelines. "Do it again, do it again, we like it, we like it." For another—and I know this is reaching wildly—it just may be that legal academics are not the best-equipped or the best-situated individuals to participate in fostering the pragmatic enterprise.

Entrenching Contradiction. Entrenching contradictions by giving them a flat ontological status is another way of denying contradiction. This approach simply makes peace with contradiction by according specific contradictions a flat, universal ontological role. Once a contradiction is universalized as intellectually intractable and historically invariant, it becomes a given, an aspect of the fixed background, the stage. No longer an actor, it loses its privileged relation to the action and is thus stripped of its creative intellectual force.

I have not seen this denial stratagem used in standard legal thought. It seems to be more popular among some CLS scholars. It is not clear to me, however, why this stance should seem appealing to CLS scholars, if it is at all. Attributing a universal ontological status to specific contradictions may appear to be radical and destabilizing (especially when everyone else worships at the altar of coherence). But despite these appearances, such depictions are likely to succeed only in enveloping contradiction in the secure stability and the comfortable coherence of the monistic form.

Sectorization. According to William James, the appropriate scholastic response to a contradiction is to make a distinction.[14] In contemporary legal thought, this response translates into the claim that if one pays sufficient respect to the jurisdictional scope—the sectors—within which ostensibly conflicting doctrines are supposed to apply, then one will find that the conflicts really are illusory. Instead, the doctrines are safely contained within their own limited fields of application.

This stratagem for the denial of contradiction seems to be a hybrid of Zeno's paradox and marginal analysis. The idea behind sectorization is that if one produces distinctions at a rate marginally faster than the production of contradiction, then the sum of these curves will always yield coherence, not contradiction. This is a great denial strategy, and it would work just fine except for one thing: it is hardly self-evident that the production of distinction and the production of contradiction are independent functions.

Theoretical Unmentionables. Theoretical unmentionables are another way of containing the recognition of contradiction within manageable proportions. Any theory or mode of thought has certain gaps, holes, and absences that, by virtue of the internal constitution of the theory or mode of thought, cannot be articulated in positive terms. Sometimes these gaps, holes, and absences bear names and thus appear to have integrity and substance, even though, by definition or by theory, nothing positive can be said about them. These, then, are *theoretical unmentionables,* those wonderful theoretical spaces that we are quite sure exist, but that by virtue of the constitution of the theory we cannot say very much about. All theories and modes of thought have them. A major distinction among theories and modes of thought, however, is how rapidly they resort to the invocation of theoretical unmentionables to resolve potential difficulties like contradiction, paradox, and incommensurability.

From this perspective, God is no doubt the all-time champion theoretical unmentionable. Featured in the same role today are some more secular derivatives including pragmatism, practical reason, good judgment, discretion, and balancing. Contradictions can be denied by referring them for resolution to the social/ conceptual space identified by these theoretical unmentionables. The unmentionables will generally work fine until one of three things happens:

1. Somebody actually tries to say something about the structure and content of these theoretical unmentionables, . . . in which case they become theoretically very mentionable. They acquire a positive content, a structural identity, and thus become subject to the very same contradictions that caused their parent discourse to produce them in the first place. Or,
2. Somebody points out that these theoretical unmentionables really are unmentionable and that accordingly, their explanatory power is, . . . well, somewhat limited. Or,
3. The theoretical unmentionables are renamed and perhaps even

reconceptualized in a way that the original purveyors of the terms do not like. Theoretical unmentionables are especially vulnerable to this sort of thing because their internal structure and content is . . . unmentionable. Just as an example: "pragmatic craft" can become "good judgment," which can become "good sense," which can become "great *karma*." The point is that the people who think they have really said something in the statement, "Mr. Justice Brandeis showed great pragmatic craft," would probably be somewhat displeased to hear this translated as "Mr. Justice Brandeis had terrific karma." But really: pragmatic craft/terrific karma—what's the difference? (It's not that there isn't any—it's just that I'd like to see it explained.)

On the whole, standard legal thought greatly underestimates the extent to which its discourses are internally contradictory, incommensurable, and paradoxical. And apart from the fact of denial, there is no great surprise or mystery about the sources of this denial. On the contrary, given the multiplicity of available contradictory discourses, denial is vastly overdetermined.

SIX

Fish v. Zapp:
The Case of the Relatively Autonomous Self

In the 1970s and 1980s, Stanley Fish was perhaps best described as an enfant terrible of American literary criticism. A scholar of Milton and speech-act theory and the author of the well-known "Is There a Text in This Class?" Fish quickly rated his own rather extensive entry in the MLA Index.

From this hardly modest beginning, Fish achieved a kind sur-disciplinary fame—causing trouble (i.e. thinking) not merely in liter-ary criticism, but in philosophy, the social sciences, and law. He built a career showing all kinds of academics (in ways that they repeatedly failed to understand) that their own academic disciplines and aca-demic projects were organized in overly imperious and thus ultimately self-defeating ways.

Fish said (and indeed continues to say) such things over and over again. Indeed, his are insights that cannot possibly be repeated enough. But Fish doesn't merely announce or even merely argue his views. He is far more vexing: he repeatedly demonstrates that the work of others, always and already, confirms his (not their) understandings of the matter. The very attempt to "read" Fish critically, analytically, etc., often ends in an uncanny reaffirmation of his views. Hence it is that the attempt to pin his work down to a professionally manageable disciplinary object—a philosophical thesis, a hermeneutic stance, a psychoanalytic technique, a rhetorical device—often meets the same infelicitous fate. That is because in all the various ways in which the various disciplines define their professionally interesting disciplinary objects, Fish's text is quite simply not there.

So much for Stanley Fish. Now for Morris Zapp. I had been told that Morris Zapp, a character in David Lodge's satire, "Changing Places," was indeed based on Stanley Fish—who had once held a position at the university in the state of Euphoria. Morris Zapp is a sort of deconstructionist extraordinaire, an intellectual bedazzler who enjoys the hell out of academic life—its give and take, its peccadilloes and its perks. He is an American bon vivant.

When I first met Stanley Fish, it was a grave shock. He did not seem like Morris Zapp at all. Fish did not have frizzy dark hair. He was not chomping on a cigar. And while he was perfectly charming, he did not exude the corpulent bonhomie of Morris Zapp.

Because this essay had already been written and, in fact, published, I became concerned that my information was wrong and that I had perpetrated a case of mistaken identity—ascribing too much reality to the wrong fiction. So I sent a copy of the essay to David Lodge. He acknowledged that indeed many people took Morris Zapp to be Stanley Fish. Lodge added, however, that he had always "thought of Morris Zapp as a relatively autonomous character," and that he was pleased that the essay that follows had clarified their "theoretical (or anti-theoretical) differences."

I am still not entirely sure.

At a conference of the University Teachers of English Language and Literature, the internationally renowned literary critic, Professor Morris Zapp, made the following comments:

To understand a message is to decode it. Language is a code. *But every decoding is another encoding.* If you say something to me I check that I have understood your message by saying it back to you in my own words, that is, different words from the ones you used, for if I repeat your own words exactly you will doubt whether I have really understood you. But if I use *my* words it follows that I have changed *your* meaning, however slightly. . . .

Reading, of course, is different from conversation. It is more passive in the sense that we can't interact with the text, we can't affect the development of the text by our own words, since the text's words are already given. That is what perhaps encourages the quest for interpretation. If the words are fixed once and for all, on the page, may not their meaning be fixed also? Not so, because the same axiom, *every decoding is another encoding,* applies to literary criticism even more stringently than it does to ordinary spoken discourse.[1]

If Professor Zapp ventured outside of literary circles to address the legal academic community, he might say something like this:

To put the matter baldly, already-in-place interpretive constructs are a condition of consciousness. It may be . . . that the thinking that goes on within them is biased (which means no more than that it has direction) but without them (a pun seriously intended) there would be no thinking at all. It follows then that the one thing you can't do in relation to interpretive constructs is choose them, and it follows too that you can't be faulted either for not having chosen them or for having chosen the wrong ones; moreover, it follows that it makes no sense to condemn as "non-rational" the reasoning that proceeds within interpretive constructs because that's the only kind of rationality there is. Finally, by the same reasoning, if you can't choose your interpretive constructs, then neither can you know them (in the sense of holding them in your hand for inspection), and if you can't know them, you can hardly be expected to take them into account when you come to explain the process by which you reached your conclusions.[2]

These comments by Stanley Fish seem to be the sort of position that Morris Zapp might take. Nonetheless, there is room for doubt. Zapp's arguments are more vertiginous than those of Fish. At bottom, when Fish is done deconstructing, he leaves us with "interpretive communities" as the comforting answer to our most taxing hermeneutical and epistemological problems. "Why is it that a constitutional provision cannot mean just anything at all?" Fish's answer is that we are "already and always" situated within "interpretive communities."[3] Zapp, by contrast, leaves us with . . . well, he leaves us with nothing at all (except, maybe, our jobs). Zapp is something of a nihilist and Fish is not.[4]

The question of interest here is what allows Fish to escape Zapp's nihilistic projection of the infinite alternation of decoding and encoding. The answer is that Fish has privileged the *relatively autonomous self*. Now, between the question and the answer, there is that small matter of getting from here to there. So, let's consider Fish's arguments.

Fish systematically deconstructs any attempt to provide foundations or formulations for interpretive activities like law. It is not possible, he argues, to give any coherent account of rules (disciplining or not)[5] or theory (moral or not)[6] that could serve to constrain interpretation. These rules or theories would themselves be texts and require interpretation.[7] Accordingly, such daring theoretical efforts cannot (and could not) regulate the practices they ostensibly address. On the contrary, theoretical production is itself a certain type of practice (an academic one) and thus stands in no special privileged relation to the judicial or legislative practices it claims to describe or regulate.[8] Fish is an absolute master at this line of argument, so this brief summary can hardly do justice to his position. But for my purposes, it is sufficient to say that as soon as Fish recognizes an element of foundationalism, essentialism, or formalism in a legal theory, he is always already well on his way toward showing that the theory does any number of embarrassingly self-defeating things.

The first move is generally to characterize an opponent (say,

Owen Fiss, Mark Kelman, Michael Moore, or Ronald Dworkin)
as saying something transcendent or privileged about law (or
whatever practice he is talking about), something like: Theory
does and should regulate practice (Dworkin).[9] Or: There really is
an ultimate reality which we should get to know in a natural
law sort of way—a way that is beyond the mere conventional
understanding (Moore).[10] Or again: It is disquieting that we
are not way more self-conscious of our interpretive constructs
(Kelman).[11] Or yet again: There are meta-rules, called "disciplining rules," that constrain the interpretation of ordinary doctrinal
rules (Fiss).[12]

From here, Fish can show that despite what the theorist claims
to provide for the practice under discussion (e.g., adjudication),
his or her contribution is really no different from—certainly, no
better than—the practice he or she is talking about. Thus, when
Fiss tried to fend off nihilism by attempting to constrain the
interpretation of legal rules (with more and better "disciplining
rules"), Fish pulled out the infinite regress. A "disciplining rule"
is still a rule. And thus Fiss's "disciplining rules" have all the same
problems as the ordinary low-level legal rules.[13] (If all texts are
indeterminate, then it's a pretty good bet (if you believe in Gödel)
that they can't be shown to be determinate with more text.)[14]

But there are other moves that Fish uses. One move, for
instance, is to show that being and thinking-about-being are two
different activities and that the latter is irrelevant to the first. (It's
not as if you can ever leave or put ontology to the side to do "pure
epistemology.") Thus, when Moore, as a natural law theorist,
claims there is an ultimate reality out there, it's not as if he could
ever step out of his being or its conventional modes of expression
to talk about what that reality looks like. So when Moore suggests that death is a natural event and that, therefore, we should
interpret statutory references to death in terms of the best scientific theory possible,[15] Fish notes that this is a cannibalistic
stance. Science, after all, is simply one conventionalist discourse
among others—no more, no less.[16]

And if, like Dworkin, our theoretical claims are more modest, we're still vulnerable. Suppose, as Dworkin does, that it would be nice (or elegant or best) for judges to make their understanding of the institutional history articulate and theoretically consistent.[17] Well, that's all fine and well, but as Fish points out, it's entirely superfluous to deciding cases. Indeed, Fish confirms what we already know—the judge (by the very fact that he or she is a judge) has already internalized that institutional history and already has the know-how to decide cases. So, as with Moore's natural law theory, it is impossible for Dworkin's theory to guide adjudication in the way he claims. Furthermore, such a theory is also quite unnecessary. If someone is already a professional (say, a judge), the last thing she needs is a theory to tell her how to think like a professional.[18]

No one seems to escape the reach of Fish's deconstruction— not even a fellow antifoundationalist like Kelman. When Kelman argues, for instance, that it is disquieting to see that interpretive constructs (like broad and narrow time frames) play a significant role in the nonrational construction of the legal world, Fish answers by pointing out that it couldn't be any other way. It is unthinkable that thinking could ever get started (much less get anywhere) if it wasn't already embedded in a situational context of interpretive constructs. Self-consciousness is fine, but the one thing it cannot do is put its interpretive constructs aside in order to choose which ones to adopt.[19]

As deconstructive moves go, Zapp would approve. When Fish is done, all that remains is a bunch of self-consuming theories. (These particular theories don't get any better until the next essay, so if you want to look there now, this would be as good a time as any.)

Indeed, by the time Fish finishes with the theorists, they are left in rather vexing predicaments. Fiss, for instance, ends up replicating the problems he started out to resolve (indeterminacy). Moore ends up appealing to that which he wants to get beyond (conventional understandings). Dworkin ends up with a theory of adjudication that cannot be used and is not necessary for his audience to do what he would like (render law pure and consistent.) Kelman's theory is irrelevant; our minds cannot achieve the impossible (transparent self-understanding).[20]

In a sense, though, the moves that Fish pulls on these theorists are one and the same. In each case, Fish has always already shown that all of these theories depend on *theoretical unmentionables* that go by the names of "interpretive communities," "interpretive assumptions and procedures," or "interpretive constructs."[21]

These artifacts are *theoretical unmentionables* in the sense that they seem to have wide-ranging explanatory power and yet they remain relatively empty and unstructured. Fish, of course, has to (and to a large extent does) keep them relatively empty and unstructured. The more Fish says about the content or structure of these theoretical unmentionables, the more he looks like he's offering a positive theory of the generation of meaning—something he denies is possible.[22] Indeed, it is a tribute to his rhetorical acuity that he can get away with saying as much as he does about the structure and content of these "interpretive communities," for as soon as Fish begins to describe them, he produces a text (maybe even the worst kind of text: a theory). And at that point, his own arguments tell us that he's just gotten it wrong: interpretive communities cannot be reduced to a text—not Fiss's text, not Dworkin's text, not even Fish's text.

Now, Fish is no doubt aware of this potential difficulty because he's extraordinarily elliptical in describing these "interpretive communities." Still, it must be hard to resist giving these things some content and structure (for otherwise who would believe that "interpretive communities" is the answer to a meaningful question?). And so, at various times, Fish's arguments can readily be taken to mean that interpretive communities or interpretive strategies really are the seat of meaning.[23] Of course, such a reading of Fish can seem disturbing. It seems to eclipse the "self" entirely, leaving it at best an empty vehicle for the reiteration of the meanings generated by interpretive communities. And not surprisingly, Fish has been criticized for annihilating the self as subject.[24] Indeed, it would be easy to go further and suggest that Fish's concept of interpretive communities has totalitarian implications in that it overwhelms both reason and the self by *appearing* to locate meaning in an ineffable and unreasoning collectivity.[25]

But Zapp would undoubtedly point out that totalitarian implications will not flow from the interpretive communities concept.[26] Zapp, I'm quite sure, would insist upon decoding the concept of "interpretive communities." In fact Zapp (who is immensely fond of flips and reversals himself) might say that Fish's approach is not totalitarian in the least because its *rhetorical* appeal presumes and depends upon something antitotalitarian: the privileging of the self.[27]

Indeed, it is the self (e.g., you, I, etc.) that knows in some no-nonsense daily-life way that Fish is right and all the Fish-bashers are wrong. What's more, the self (yours, mine, etc.) knows this against the rules of construction, against theory, and against reason itself. The self knows that there is something irreducible about the act of interpretation that simply cannot be made articulate, and that in any case could not be captured by anything so systematic, so universal, or so univocal as a theory. The self knows that interpretation is a social practice and that there will always be something about practice that cannot be reduced to rules, theory, or reason.

Of course, it is not just any self that knows this. It is not the biblical self—if it were, Fish would be talking about God rather than interpretive communities. Nor is it the Hegelian self—if it were, Fish would be talking about the dialectics of the self-conscious subject in history. Nor is it the Kantian self—for if it were, Fish would not be talking about interpretive communities at all. No, this is a situated self—a relatively autonomous twentieth-century self that readily accepts the influence of social context and social convention in the construction and interpretation of daily life. This is a self that has survived the onslaughts of Freud, Marx, and all the other moderns.

One might think that this is an impoverished embattled self—constantly retreating in the face of advances by modernist theory and positivist social science. But actually, it is a rather clever, imperious self. While it concedes that it is only *relatively* autonomous, cunningly it makes this concession cut against the claims of reason and theory—even history. Social science may have its uses and modern theory its moments, but, at bottom, it is the self that understands (and can be trusted to understand) what is really going on. Accordingly, the relatively autonomous self (yours, mine, etc.) maintains full rights to determine the scope and boundaries of its own autonomy.

Of course, one might wonder why this self should be enthralled by Fish's concept of interpretive communities. After all, the concept of interpretive communities is the linchpin in an approach that deconstructs the myth of radical subjectivism. And what could be more flattering to the self than a radical subjectivism? Well . . . actually . . . lots of things. Radical subjectivism (like radical objectivism) is too threatening to the relatively autonomous self. The former places far too much responsibility (moral and otherwise) on the self and leaves it far too contingent.[28] Radical objectivism, on the other hand, leaves the self too constrained and rather hollow.[29]

But Fish is just right. For the relatively autonomous self, Fish offers the best of all possible worlds. What's more, Fish allows the self to claim that it is right when it insists on acting or deciding in an intuitionistic pragmatic sort of way. The self can say, "Yes, I know your theory of [. . .] requires that I should do such and such, but you see I am not a theorist; I am a self and I know things in an intuitionistic nontheoretical practical way which your theory could not possibly understand. So go away—go do your theory (which is just a form of practice anyway) and let me get on with my business." The concept of interpretive communities is attractive for the simple reason that it leaves the self as the final adjudicator of its own acts without responsibility for the choice. The self cannot choose its interpretive constructs. It is always already within them. But at the same time (and quite conveniently), very little can be known about these interpretive constructs, so the self need not feel closeted by an overly determined objectivity. The concept of interpretive communities offers the self *a formal closure* against the claims of theory, reason, and history. But at the same time, the concept is *substantively empty*, so that the self can project into "interpretive communities" just about anything it wants.

This is an incredibly flattering picture for the relatively autonomous self—and Fish is the first to point it out:

> According to the position presented here, no one can claim privilege for the point of view he holds and therefore everyone is obliged to practice the art of persuasion. This includes me, and persuasion is the art that I have been trying to practice here. . . . In general, people resist what you have to say when it seems to them to have undesirable or even disastrous consequences. . . . In short, I have been trying to persuade you to believe what I believe because it is in your own best interests as *you* understand them. In short my message . . . is finally not challenging, but consoling—not to worry.
>
> My fiction is liberating. It relieves me of the obligation to be right (a standard that simply drops out) and demands only that I be interesting (a standard that can be met without any reference at all to an illusory objectivity). Rather than restoring or recovering texts, I am in the business of making texts and of teaching others to make them by adding to their repertoire of strategies.[30]

Of course, the mere fact that the rhetorical appeal of Fish's approach is addressed to the relatively autonomous self hardly means that Fish's work depends on that self. Still, absent a privileging of the relatively autonomous self, it is hard to see why Fish's account would be so compelling. To be sure, his arguments against foundationalism, essentialism, and formalism are well taken. But what makes the concept of interpretive communities or institutional communities or interpretive constructs so appealing? Why should we believe in interpretive communities any more than we should believe in authorial intent, the text, God, or little space people from Mars? In other words, why doesn't the infinite regress and the other arguments Fish launches against foundationalism and essentialism and formalism go on and on and on . . . right through the floor of interpretive communities? After so much gleeful smashing of such heavy-duty hitters as Fiss, Dworkin, Kelman, and Moore, it comes as some surprise to see Fish leave any text intact. And yet in his own text, Fish leaves some rather major dichotomies still standing:

rules/context
theory/practice
thinking/being
text/interpretive community.[31]

For Fish, the left-hand terms of the dichotomies can never get it right. They can never overcome the boundary (the "/") to control or inform the right-hand terms. And that is because the left-hand terms are always already embedded in the right-hand terms. If Fish's account is right, then context can never be reduced to a set of rules (Fiss's problem); practice can never be subservient to theory (Dworkin's difficulty); and epistemology will always already be outdone by being (Kelman and Moore's shortfall). The short of it is: interpretive communities simply cannot be read like a text. Now, this is rather determinate stuff for an antiformalist like Fish, and thus it prompts the question: "Why stop the deconstruction here?"

Even if one can't find a good philosophical answer to this

question (and Fish would be the first to say that one can't), there is, nonetheless, a damned good rhetorical answer. The answer is that the relatively autonomous self is more than happy to stop the deconstructive ride, and the interpretive community thesis is a better place to get off than most.

The concept of interpretive communities is alluring precisely because it describes what the relatively autonomous self intuitively discovers when it is thinking about its own condition. The self realizes that it is always already operating within a context of interpretive practice that it has not chosen and cannot fully articulate. What's more, it realizes that there seems to be a certain regularity to practices such as baseball or constitutional interpretation, but one which cannot be described in a way that captures the thing itself. It realizes, in short, that it is relatively autonomous. But apart from these insights (courtesy of the relatively autonomous self), Fish has given us no reason to believe in interpretive communities or institutional communities or interpretive constructs. Of course, that's precisely his point—if he had given us an ultimate reason to believe in interpretive communities, he would have failed (by his own account). Why then do we believe Fish when he tells us that it all hinges on "interpretive communities?" For the relatively autonomous self, the answer is easy: one always already does.

It is at this point, I think, that Zapp's approach would break decisively with that of Fish. If "every decoding is another encoding," then surely Zapp would insist upon decoding this concept of the relatively autonomous self. After all, if the seemingly totalitarian concept of interpretive communities can lead to the relatively autonomous self in less than twelve pages, one must wonder about the integrity of that self.

When the relatively autonomous self buys into the concept of interpretive communities, it seems to be cutting a pretty good deal: one that enshrines the self as the ultimate adjudicator of the nature of reality, and one which reprieves it of responsibility for the choice. "It's not me," the self can say, "I am always already situated in an interpretive community and I do not choose my interpretive constructs." And very quietly, the relatively autonomous self whispers to itself, "Yes, that's right—I do not choose my interpretive constructs and neither does history or reason or anything else that could displace me."

Of course, the relatively autonomous self (as its name indicates) is not entirely stable. Being only *relatively* autonomous, it is constantly called upon to adjudicate the boundaries of its own autonomy. Indeed, it is constantly being seduced or bullied into accepting some insuperable subjectivism or some intolerable objectivism. This constant struggle against such philosophical and rhetorical threats can lead the relatively autonomous self to ask itself some strange questions. It can ask, for instance, how it knows what it is doing. The answer is that the self doesn't really know what it is doing, because it is embedded in interpretive constructs that it cannot know about. It just sort of groks[32] its way through life. If the self did know what it was doing, it wouldn't be relatively autonomous anymore: it wouldn't be autonomous at all, but instead subject to some rule or theory (which it could know).

Having admitted that it cannot know what it is doing, the relatively autonomous self might begin to wonder just what it is that keeps it together as a unified, more or less stable, and generally continuous entity throughout the day. The answer is that the relatively autonomous self is kept whole by a meaning structure which, of course, is always already embedded in interpretive communities.[33] You see—nothing to worry about. Of course, the relatively autonomous self might ask how it can be sure that indeed, the interpretive communities are not God (or something else) forbid, self-destructive—perhaps cannibalistic? And the answer, of course, is that the self cannot be sure because, again, it is always already embedded in interpretive communities whose structure and contents cannot be known. It is these unknowable interpretive communities that keep the self stable and contented. The relatively autonomous self knows that these interpretive communities are benign and stable. They are stable, aren't they?

At this point, the relatively autonomous self may begin to feel insecure. For one thing, Fish's interpretive community thesis offers no reason to suppose that these interpretive communities are benign. For another, the relatively autonomous self is beginning to realize that whenever difficult questions about the status and structure of the self are raised, the relatively autonomous self always privileges itself: it always establishes itself as the prime adjudicator. Call it instinct, good judgment, or pragmatism—it doesn't matter: it is always the relatively autonomous self that comes out on top. After reading Fish, however, the relatively autonomous self realizes that this is a questionable and, ironically, foundationalist move. The relatively autonomous self realizes that if it believes in interpretive communities, there is no reason (other than solipsism) to privilege itself.[34] And if there is no reason for the relatively autonomous self to privilege itself, there is no reason to believe in "interpretive communities" or "interpretive strategies" or in any other version of the *theoretical unmentionables*.

The reason is simple: if they are *theoretical unmentionables,* then the one thing you can't do with them (absent a stunning display of bad faith) is talk about what they look like. You can't talk about whether they are clans, or cabals, or democratic institutions, or efficient firms, or illegitimate hierarchies or .... This sort of constraint, exclusion, ground rule (whatever you want to call it) can really put a crimp in a conversation about the content and structure of social life. And at this point, I think this is one conversation the relatively autonomous self won't want to miss— if only to figure out who it really is and what in the world keeps it that way—if anything.

Fish's interpretive community thesis *seems* to interrupt this conversation about the content and structure of social life. Yet, absent the bad faith of the relatively autonomous self, his thesis neither can nor should interrupt this conversation. Indeed, either the interpretive community thesis places no constraints on this conversation (in which case, according to Fish, the thesis is irrelevant), or it does contribute some constraints to this conversation (in which case, according to Fish, it must be wrong). There are, of course, worse things than being wrong:[35] one of them is commitment to a belief that shuts down understanding when there is nothing necessary about that belief.

Ironically, it is Zapp's scholarship that will serve as the last example. It turns out that Zapp (like Fish) is not quite the deconstructionist he first appears to be. Indeed, Zapp would find no reason to believe in the interpretive community thesis offered by Fish, because no point on the infinite alternation of encoding and decoding is worth believing. One commentator, who was quite distressed by the implications of this position, asked Zapp what the point of academic literary studies might be? Zapp responded:

> The point, of course, is to uphold the institution of academic literary studies. We maintain our position in society by publicly performing a certain ritual, just like any other group of workers in the realm of discourse—lawyers, politicians, journalists. And as it looks as if we have done our duty for today, shall we all adjourn for a drink?[36]

Now, as welcome as Zapp's invitation may be to his audience, his position remains impossible, untenable, not to mention, unappealing.

Conclusion

Fish is persuasive, extremely persuasive, way too much so. He's even right (except, of course, about interpretive communities and the like). Zapp is useful, but wrong (not to mention unreal).[37] And I'm not too sure about the relatively autonomous self.

That's it—except for a few concluding remarks:

1. The relatively autonomous self is a relatively accurate description of the modern self.[38]
2. The relatively autonomous self is a fiction. It has no solidity.
Its only substance is contingent.
3. You can read just about anything you want into the relatively
autonomous self if you are one (and maybe even if you
aren't)—except that . . .
4. Any claims you might make about the *real* meaning or *real*
nature of the relatively autonomous self are always already
off the mark because the structure and role of the relatively
autonomous self doesn't allow you to make such claims. And
that's because . . .
5. The relatively autonomous self is (among other things) a language game.
6. It is a language game that has an uncanny similarity to Fish's
interpretive community thesis. Indeed, the relatively autonomous self is a reflection in the mirror of the self of the
formal configurations and the substantive emptiness of Fish's
interpretive communities. Indeed, all the points above about
the relatively autonomous self have some application to Fish's
interpretive communities.
7. There is no reason to believe in interpretive communities or
in the relatively autonomous self. And as I've suggested, there
are good reasons not to.
8. The relatively autonomous self is unstable and structured to
become something else. The question is, what?
9. To answer this question, it would be useful to historicize the
character and structure of what Fish sometimes refers to as
"interpretive communities." But that has become very difficult—not because of Fish's arguments per se, but rather because of the underlying character of the social practices that
make his interpretive-community thesis seem plausible (even
appealing) to so many different kinds of people. I am referring
to bureaucratic forms of life: the refinement, expansion, and
increasing rationalization of the bureaucratic form is not so-

cially (or intellectually) weightless. Over time, it yields the accelerating mutability of meaning, the increased insularity and specialization of knowledges, the heightened instrumentalization of cultural symbols and values, the fetishism of instrumentalism, and the proliferation of complexity and fragmentation. In that sort of world, the interpretive-community thesis can seem at once sensible and comforting. In fact, it is neither.

The final score is in the next essay.

Theory and the Uses of Dennis Martinez

Fish recently began a law review article with a story about Dennis Martinez, then a pitcher for the Baltimore Orioles. Ira Berkow, a reporter, saw Dennis Martinez talking to his manager, Earl Weaver, before a game. Sensing a story, Berkow approached Martinez and asked him "what words of wisdom had been imparted" by Weaver. Dennis Martinez answered, "'Throw strikes and keep 'em off the bases' and I said O.K. . . . What else could I say? What else could he say?"[39]

Fish would like us to believe that it would have been inappropriate for Weaver to say anything else. And maybe that's true. It's hard to know: Stanley Fish is in some sense (a very limited sense) an outsider to baseball. But he's no outsider to theory. He knows how to craft a story—particularly a good philosophical story—one that resonates deeply in the culture. And given the sort of attacks Fish makes on Fiss, Dworkin, Kelman, and others, I don't have any doubts about it: outsider or not, if Fish were manager of the Orioles, he would have had plenty to say to Dennis Martinez on the night of the game.

For instance, as Dennis Martinez's manager, Fish could have said something like this: "O.K., Dennis, I'm gonna make a lot of changes tonight: pinch hitters, substitutions, the whole ball of wax. But like I said last time, don't start reading meaning into any of this. It'll just mess you up. So if I'm screaming at the ump, that's all I'm doing: screaming at the ump—nothing more, nothing less. So don't go looking for signs about signs about signs. This game is about throwing strikes. You don't need to be reading signs about signs in order to do that. You understand what I'm saying? Just go out there and do it, champ." Now, Fish could say this. In fact, this is sort of what he told Fiss and Dworkin. It's also somewhat reminiscent of what Wittgenstein told us when he suggested that ultimately all rules, reasons, and theories are situated in a form of life.[40]

But Fish could have said other things. He could have said, for instance: "All right, champ, it's going to be a long game—you know that and I know that. Now, I know that at various points you'll be sitting in the dugout or maybe standing on the mound, just waiting and thinking. You can think about the game all you want. In fact, I want you to. In fact, you know I want you to. But like I've told you before, don't think for one moment that you can ever step outside the game to think about it. If things go into a slump, don't get frazzled—it's just a bad moment. It's gonna be a long game—and the way it looks at any particular moment is not necessarily the way it will look at the end. Now, go out there and may Geist be with you." This speech has a certain similarity to what Fish told Moore, the natural law theorist. And it bears at least some similarity to Hegel's message about the historical situatedness of consciousness.

Not to be overlooked are all the Kantian possibilities: "O.K., champ—this game is all psych. You know that and I know that. And you've got psych—it's written all over you . . . in an a priori sort of way. There's no way you could throw those fastballs and those curves if you didn't always already have psych. Hell, in your case it's a transcendental cinch that you've got it. And no amount of self-doubt or introspection can take that away from you. 'Cause you can never step out of your own psych. You're always within your own psych. So, don't worry about a thing—no matter how things are going, you've got the stuff that'll get us through." This is the sort of story that Fish pulls on Kelman—to keep him from asking for the impossible.

Now, you may have noticed that these little speeches don't gain much in the way of authority from my explicit articulation of their philosophical origins. Fish knows this: he wouldn't go around mucking up his instructions to Dennis Martinez with citations to these philosophical heavies. It's neither useful nor necessary. Hell, it's even dangerous. Can you imagine Dennis Martinez saying, "Wow, did Hegel really say that? Does Wittgenstein agree?"

So, while aspects of Fish's rhetoric at times seem to draw on various philosophers—traces of Kant, Hegel, or Wittgenstein—he doesn't really need these fellows. On the other hand (and this is the important part), that their basic moves and narrative lines are deeply ensconced in the culture certainly doesn't hurt Fish any. You might say that the audience is prepared—or, in Fish's terms, we have always already heard it before (and in the oddest places). And just in case we haven't, Fish will tell a story or two beforehand to get us in the right frame of mind—for instance, stories about baseball, industrial research, or graduate students. This rhetorical procedure, of course, tracks the substance of what Fish has to say: we are always already operating in the tracks of the preconceptions and interpretive presumptions that Fish has constructed with his stories.[41] So by the time you read Fish's account of Kelman or Dworkin, or whoever, it *seems* like you always already know why they're wrong and it *feels* like you don't even need Fish to help you at all. But you do—and he has. Still, if Fish doesn't need philosophy to make his point, what does he need?

If you look closely at Fish's arguments, he needs something like the inside/outside distinction. Throwing strikes and keeping 'em off the bases is what Dennis Martinez is supposed to do. It's the *inner* game of baseball. Dennis Martinez doesn't need instructions to do that. Anything a news reporter might say to analyze Martinez's performance might well be interesting to sports fans, but it is always already *outside* the *inner* game.

The same is true of discourse about a practice and the practice itself. The theory of that practice is always already *outside* of that practice and *inside* its own practice. Dennis Martinez knows that. If you don't, and if, like Moore, you think you can figure out how Dennis Martinez pitches by thinking about the real Dennis Martinez, Fish will get you. There is no way of thinking or talking about the real Dennis Martinez other than the conventional ways furnished by history. There may be a "real" essence of Dennis Martinez, but you are always already going to be *outside* of it because you will always be within your own conventional understanding. And if, like Kelman, you think that you should choose the way you think (your interpretive constructs) more carefully so you don't miss what Dennis Martinez is really doing on the mound, Fish will get you again. You can't choose your interpretive constructs because you are always already *within* them. And if you were *without* them, you couldn't think about baseball or anything else. If all this still concerns you, and, like Dworkin, you think that it would be nice (or best, or most elegant) to make the way you think about baseball articulate and consistent, Fish will get you again. Articulating even the best theory of the institutional history of baseball is something that is always already *outside* that practice. And if what you're interested in is telling baseball players how to play, they don't need (and couldn't use) your theory.

Indeed, no matter what you do (or what you think) Fish will get you every time—as long, of course, as you allow him that crucial move: the establishment of the inside/outside distinction. It's that sort of distinction and its analogues (within/without, within/with, here/beyond, dependent/independent, and one thing/and another) that allow Fish to confound theory, rules, self-reflection, and ultimate truth (maybe even God) every time. The latter are always on the outs with Fish. They are always *outside* of what they are discussing or attempting to do because they are always *within* their own practice, being, context, etc. Indeed, Fish is the first to tell you this: "A theory, in short, is something a practitioner consults when he wishes to perform correctly, with the term 'correctly' here understood as meaning independently of his preconceptions, biases, or personal preferences."[42] You may have noticed that this definition already places theory *outside* practice. But the definition does substantially more than that: it already places theory *outside* the realm of possibility. Indeed, the sentence cannibalizes itself: it is never the case (and indeed could not ever be the case) that a practitioner *wishes* to consult something (anything) *independently* of his or her preconceptions, biases, or personal preferences.

Thus, it's not so much theory in particular that is impossible, but anything that Fish wants to insert in that first sentence, "A _____ , in short, is something a practitioner consults when he wishes to perform. . . ." Try it—everything turns out to be impossible: a coach, a counselor, a judge, a timetable, the Koran, art—whatever.[43] With this definition, Fish has set up a formal language game which theory (or anything else) must necessarily fail. It's thus a stunning display of intellectual modesty when Fish says of theory, "I reserve that word for an abstract or algorithmic formulation that guides or governs practice from a position outside any particular conception of practice."[44] Why pick just on abstract or algorithmic formulations?

If philosophy is mute on this issue (or if it says too many things at once) there is, nonetheless, a pretty good rhetorical answer. Theorists *seem to* claim that their enterprise is somehow entitled to greater authority than all the others. (And even when they don't, it's easy enough to make them look like they do.) Fish argues that when legal theorists claim that they know the practice that they are discussing, their texts generally give the hint that the theories are somehow outside or beyond or above the practice being discussed. Fish's use of this inside/outside distinction is not all that difficult: the typical English sentence (the sort used by theorists) usually has a subject doing something (by way of a verb) to a direct object. Thus, in one sense, the subject is always *outside* the direct object. Now, if the subject is theory and the object is practice, there is a sense in which never the twain shall meet. It is, thus, no surprise that theorists talk as though theory governs practice, or as if theory addresses an ultimate reality beyond practice. Or as if thought itself can trump being.

Now, I don't think this is theory per se. I think it's just bad theory (or simply a bad reading of theory). But in either case, this image of theory enables Fish to come in (ironically from the outside) and (ironically like a theorist) to inscribe some troublesome inside/outside distinctions into the text of theory. Fish can turn just about any legal theorist on his or her head by simply showing that the theorist (despite what he or she says) rather self-defeatingly asserts that his or her

> theory is outside practice
> rules are outside context
> texts are outside interpretive communities
> thinking is outside being.

And we are accustomed to believing Fish when he makes this claim, because that's the way we usually think of legal theory and legal theorists.

In one sense this observation seems to corroborate Fish's point. If we are accustomed to looking at theory this way, and, more important, if theorists are apt to write theory this way, Fish's interpretive-community thesis must be correct after all. Well ... no. One can acknowledge that practice, context, interpretive communities, and being (on the one hand) have some (even a significant) relation to theory, rules, texts, and thinking (on the other) and yet avoid describing the relation of the two in terms of hard-edged images such as the inside/outside distinction. If one abandons this sort of hard-edged image, theory, rules, texts, and thinking again become relevant to the understanding and critique of practice (and all that other stuff).[45] Now, you'll notice that in the previous sentence I've just done what I said I didn't want to do. If you look at that sentence, it seems I've reinscribed a hard edge between theory on the one side and practice on the other. And that's one possible reading of the sentence. It is the sort of reading (and the sort of sentence) that Fish would seize upon to show that my position is self-consuming. But despite the fact that Fish can always already read my sentence in this way, and even offer you very persuasive reasons to read it this way, there's one thing that he can't do, and that is *exclude* a more interesting, more complex reading of the sentence—which is, I hope, what I have just done.

The point is that the hermeneutic and linguistic and Marxist arguments that theory is always already situated do not argue against the relevance, use, or need of theory. Rather, they are merely arguments about what theory is and should be. And they're pretty good ones: too good to be formalized under the rubric of "interpretive communities" and the *closure* it imposes.

Indeed, the "interpretive communities" thesis achieves closure too soon. In fact, Fish is the first to tell you so in his recent essay. Fish thinks there is a lesson in the interchange between Martinez and his manager, Weaver: "What they know is either inside them of them or (at least on this day) beyond them; and if they know it, they did not come to know it by submitting to a formalization; neither can any formalization capture what they know in such a way as to make it available to those who haven't come to know it in the same way." [46] Now, this rendition of the "interpretive community" thesis is something of a *self-consuming* statement. If what Martinez and Weaver know is not subject to formalization, then it certainly isn't subject to the formalization that it isn't subject to formalization.

The score isn't in on theory (or law, for that matter). As for that *other* game Fish talks about, Martinez, Weaver and the rest of the Orioles lost to the Yankees, five to four. [47]

SEVEN

How to Do Things with the First Amendment

This is an essay about law, speech, rhetoric and fetishism (with special attention to "The First Amendment"). It was first delivered as a comment on Stanley Fish's presentation of "Fraught with Death: Skepticism, Progressivism, and the First Amendment."

> The fading away of [X] is signaled not by silence but by more and more talk, more journals, more symposia, and more entries in the contest for the right to sum up [X]'s story. There will come a time when it is a contest no one will want to win, when the announcement of still another survey of [X] is received not as a promise but as a threat, and when the calling of still another conference on the function of [X] in our time will elicit only a groan. That time may have come: [X]'s day is dying; the hour is late; and the only thing left for a [student of X] is to say so, which is what I have been saying here, and, I think not a moment too soon.
>
> —STANLEY FISH (AS MODIFIED BY THE AUTHOR),
> *Consequences* (1985)

I am not here to criticize Stanley Fish's presentation. I am here to interpret it. I am not here to defend or to criticize the First

Amendment. In an important sense, I won't have much to say about the First Amendment at all.

Now, you're probably thinking: he can't do that. This is a conference on the First Amendment. He's got to talk about the First Amendment. Well, yes. And in a way, I will. But as I see it, all this talk about "The First Amendment" is no more about the First Amendment than fear of stepping on a crack in the sidewalk is about sidewalks. The First Amendment here is, in all sorts of ways, the sidewalk. And I'm not interested in sidewalks. And so, I will have absolutely nothing to say about where the cracks should be located on the First Amendment sidewalk, or whether they should be moved or why, or anything of the sort. What I want to talk about is what Stanley Fish is doing and how he does it.

So is Stanley Fish right about the First Amendment? Of course, he is right. He is right from a certain perspective. And his rightness, of course, must itself be an interested partisan perspective — namely, his own. Now, to call Stanley Fish's perspective an interested partisan one is not an objection, much less a refutation of his argument. It is, rather, as he might say, its restatement.

So what has Stanley Fish been doing here? He has been doing what all legal thinkers strive to do when they talk and write about the First Amendment. What they do — within the limits of their capacities and their agendas — is try to make "The First Amendment" their own. They are all, in other words, busily composing their own version of that famous, apocryphal, but utterly emblematic piece of scholarship: "What the First Amendment Means to me." They are all, as they "edify," "clarify," "expand," or "contract" the First Amendment, trying to inscribe their own politics, their own agendas into the First Amendment.

Now, to this claim, there is, of course, an immediate objection. The objection is that while some legal thinkers are clearly projecting their fondest, indeed sometimes florid, hopes into the First Amendment, there are many others who seem to show an

utterly subservient and reverential attitude for the First Amendment and its demands. Think here of a certain kind of First
Amendment purist or a doctrinally chastened legal thinker. These
thinkers and their subservience are readily identifiable because
you will see them routinely offer up their own cherished political commitments as sacrifices on the altar of the First Amendment.

This desire for self-abnegation, for self-denial before a higher
power, is familiar. It is what we call, in ethics, self-mastery; in
theology, worship; in psychoanalysis, masochism; and in jurisprudence, legal process. Those who strive so hard to submit their
writings and their talks to the exigent and intransigent commands
of the First Amendment are seeking to be *bound,* and this desire
for bondage—and we must use that word, for it is the word *they*
use—this too is an interested perspective. And its interested
character becomes quite obvious, when one realizes that this
desire for bondage is meant for export. It is then what we call, in
ethics, mastery over others; in theology, proselytizing; in psychoanalysis, sadism; and in jurisprudence, legal process.

This desire for bondage to a higher law is, of course, eminently
understandable. I'll skip the ethical, theological, psychoanalytic
accounts and go straight for the jurisprudence. This desire for
bondage to a higher law is what gives legal thinkers perhaps
what they desire most: the sense that they actually "know" something and that what they know actually has some power. What
they know they call "reason," and what they want is for reason to
be in charge of power. This, of course, is the standard-issue
liberal enlightenment dream. (I won't deal here with its Marxian
twin.) What many legal thinkers want is for the dream to come
true.

The premium juridical test site for the dream—the laboratory,
as it were—is the First Amendment. It is the key site, because it
presents the challenge in its purest form and, at least at first
glance, its easiest form. Thus, it might be said of the liberal

enlightenment thinker and the First Amendment exactly the
inverse of what is said about New York: if you cannot make it
here, you cannot make it anywhere.

Among the many things that the First Amendment offers to
the liberal enlightenment thinker is the opportunity to work out
some key liberal enlightenment distinctions. Now, some of these
key distinctions appear in Stanley Fish's presentation; others do
not. But it doesn't matter much because, in the jurisprudential
lore of the First Amendment, these distinctions are all, for most
purposes, variations on each other. They are all homologies of
the liberal enlightenment attempt to distinguish reason and
power. The key homologous distinctions mentioned in Stanley
Fish's paper are

speech   action
free speech   consequential speech
constative utterance   performative utterance[1]

We could add others to the list, such as:

expression   action
communication   conduct
persuasion   coercion

Anyone wanting to press the point will immediately see that
all these distinctions are also variations on the mind/body distinction—a distinction that Fish does not mention explicitly in his
presentation, but nonetheless exploits ruthlessly through the strategic use of adjectives—"bloodless" being, I think, the most
memorable.

Now, what makes the First Amendment challenging for the
liberal enlightenment thinker is that some such distinction must
be made to define the scope of the First Amendment, and it must
be made from a perspective or a place that is itself free and not

consequential, a place that is itself persuasion and not coercion, a place that is [. . .] and not [. . .]. Stanley Fish describes the strategies used to describe that place. The distinctions are familiar: the place must be

neutral	not interested
universal	not particular
public	not private
law	not politics
truth	not experience

In Stanley Fish's argument, all these distinctions—both the first and the second set—bite the dust. And they bite the dust in all the usual ways—ways that I have somewhat uncharitably identified in terms that are also *fraught with death.*

The first of Stanley Fish's moves is the least interesting, because it is the most common. It is the least used in Fish's argument. It is:

1. Radical Perspectivalism. This move is used by Fish to show that any attempt to draw the critical enlightenment First Amendment distinctions must recognize that these distinctions are always drawn from some point of view. The next step is to point out that there are indeed many points of view, and that the identity of the critical distinctions depends upon the point of view whence they are drawn. But this cannot be (or so the argument goes), because the very identity of the critical distinctions also requires that they cannot be drawn from a particular point of view.

2. Suicidal Conceptual Purification. This move serves to render the enlightenment distinctions impossible. Stanley Fish argues that in order to be able to discharge their functions, the categories of reason (free speech or truth or whatever) must be demarcated

as completely separate from their opposing terms. But thus purified of interest, desire, agenda, program, or any of the other terms
that could supply *motivation*, these categories of reason turn out
to be utterly empty. In Fish's own words, they are "formal,"
"thin," "substanceless," "bodiless," "empty," "bloodless," and "abstract." They have, in Ronald Dworkin's telling invocation of the
well-worn phrase, worked themselves pure—so pure, in fact, that
nothing remains.[2] Total purification means total emptiness. And
being utterly empty, such disembodied free speech and free
speech values cannot produce anything nor contain anything of
value. They have become like Gertrude Stein's Oakland: there is
no there there.

3. Transitive Conceptual Contamination. Not surprisingly, Fish
insists that these totally purified categories are impossible. They
are impossible because they could only be created from an interested, partisan, political perspective. In other words, these purified categories either do not exist or they are fatally contaminated
by desire, politics, interest, and so on. And, of course, true to
the metaphor of contamination they are not just a little bit
contaminated. Contamination is not a matter of degree—at least
not from the perspective of the party contaminated. To give an
example: When Stanley Fish following Robert Post following
Frank Easterbrook following Catharine MacKinnon recognizes
that *pornographic speech* has a performative (nonreasoning) dimension, he, like all the others, is led to acknowledge that *all speech*
has a performative dimension.[3] The point is that once the contamination starts, it is contamination all the way through. That
is because, as Fish would have it, there is no uncontaminated
place from which to draw an uncontaminated line. Once contaminated with the guilty knowledge, paradise is lost, and there's just
no way of getting back.

In First Amendment jurisprudence, the guilty knowledge is
precisely this knowledge that all speech has a performative di-

mension. It is the knowledge that merely in speaking, something is already being done. This is dangerous knowledge. It is expressed periodically in the academic literature (and then forgotten over and over again). Indeed, before Catharine MacKinnon, Frank Easterbrook, Robert Post, Stanley Fish, and now I, and indeed now *you*, were led to recognize that all speech has a performative dimension, the point had been articulated by John Hart Ely.

Ely had been confronting a rather popular theory of the time which divided the realm of human behavior into two purportedly distinct categories: action and expression. This was the theory advanced by Thomas Emerson, who argued that while "action" was not protected by the First Amendment, "expression" was.[4] I remember this theory well, because at the time I was a law student taking the First Amendment course. I thought Emerson had developed a truly great theory—one with obvious economizing virtues. I was hoping the theory would hold up. But it was not to be. Indeed, Emerson's theory had already been dealt a death blow in 1975, when John Hart Ely succinctly pointed out, in reference to the *O'Brien*[5] case, that draft card burning "is an undifferentiated whole, 100% action and 100% expression. It involves no conduct that is not at the same time communication, and no communication that does not result from conduct."[6]

And of course, in accordance with the logic of transitive conceptual contamination, it turned out that this truth about draft card burning became a truth about symbolic speech in general—and then about speech in general. Indeed, in the very movement from John Hart Ely's textual comments respecting *O'Brien* to his supporting footnote, we already have an amplification of the point.[7] So the transitive conceptual contamination proceeds apace: what is true of burning of draft cards becomes true of symbolic speech becomes true of all speech.

Now, while this point has epidemic implications difficult to cabin, it is also the sort of point that is forgotten *over and over again* in the academic First Amendment literature. It is a point which, in order for standard liberal First Amendment literature to sustain itself, *must be* forgotten over and over again. Indeed, forgetting this point is a precondition to doing standard liberal First Amendment thought. To put it another way, if you are the sort of person who cannot tell the difference between action and expression or their substitute homologies, you simply cannot do standard liberal First Amendment thought. This, as Stanley Fish might say, is a condition devoutly to be wished for; and if you can hold on to it, it's yours.

Now, this, I think, sets forth the broad outlines of Stanley Fish's argumentative strategy. Notice what Fish has done here. He has represented (and in a sense, quite accurately, I think) the liberal enlightenment First Amendment in its prototypical object-forms: sharp lines, boundaries, stable identities, etc. As the two lists above reveal, this liberal enlightenment First Amendment is very clear, very neat, very stable, very static. Meanwhile, the world which Stanley Fish fashions for this highly objectified First Amendment is very much an animated one. It is a world animated according to some rather peculiar poststructuralist logics: including, as I have called them, radical perspectivalism, suicidal conceptual purification, and transitive conceptual contamination.

Now, in a world that is characterized by these somewhat unfriendly logics, the attempt to construct a box around whatever it is one values—say, free speech, for instance—is as eminently understandable as it is ill-advised. There is a deathly—indeed a suicidal—asymmetry here. And this asymmetry manifests itself in three problems.

The first problem might be called the problem of *recognition*. Basically, the problem is that standard-issue enlightenment liberalism is just not equipped to understand the sort of world it is dealing with here. It won't even know where it is, much less how it got here or how the hell to get out. Very likely it won't even recognize that it is in serious intellectual trouble.[8] It won't even realize when it has made a faux pas. In short, in this world, it doesn't have a chance. Now, if this seems too alarmist, or if you have absolutely no idea what I am talking about, that just proves my point exactly. Indeed, given the sort of poststructuralist animation in Stanley Fish's text, it is a stone-cold cinch that the clumsy objectifications of the liberal enlightenment First Amendment will have a life that is nasty, brutish, and short. Indeed, its life is over before it even begins.

The second problem is one of *identity*. In Fish's text, the First Amendment is constantly searching for a place to be—a place beyond rhetoric, beyond politics. It is looking for a place where neutrality is just neutrality, truth is just truth, and so on. But in Stanley Fish's world (and, perhaps more vexingly, in yours too, it turns out) there is no such place—not in the past, not in the present, and not in the future. And if there were (which there isn't), you couldn't get to it from here anyway. The ontology won't allow for it. The construction of the field in terms of radical perspectivalism, suicidal conceptual purification, and transitive conceptual contamination ensure that there is never a coincidence between the description of identity and identity itself. Dislocation is the ontological rule. Violation of the rule means coming to rest. And coming to rest means death.

The third problem is one of *motivation*. The liberal enlightenment First Amendment couldn't move itself even if it wanted to. But, of course, it doesn't want to. And it doesn't want to because it has real motivation problems. The problem is that the liberal enlightenment First Amendment is just like an object. And being just like an object, this First Amendment has no ability to move itself. Instead, it is utterly dependent upon, and captive to, external forces for movement and direction; hence it is subject to the implosion produced through suicidal conceptual purification, the perpetual displacement effected through transitive conceptual contamination, and the erratic dislocations prompted by radical perspectivalism.

INTERLUDE

Now, for those who are interested in criticizing Fish's argument, there is no doubt some mileage to be gained by focusing attention on the way that his constitutive object-form metaphors have boxed the liberal enlightenment vision of the First Amendment into a highly stable object-form, while his animated description of the world in which the First Amendment must operate is fraught with motion, movement, change, and so on. Now, of course, before you pursue this line of criticism, you might want to consider whether these liberal enlightenment First Amendment boxes that Stanley Fish has evoked are yours as well. And if these are also your boxes, now would be a really good time to wonder why and how it is that you are so fond of boxes. Not to put too fine a point on it, but why remain so attached to boxes even in the midst of an article whose very title reads, "*Fraught with Death:* [. . .], [. . .], and [. . .]"? I have some answers to this question, but it would be unseemly to present them here.[9]

END OF INTERLUDE

Now, to get back to the main action: Is Stanley Fish here merely ganging up on enlightenment liberalism or the First Amendment? I don't think so. He's doing much more than that. What he is doing here is exploiting—and I don't mean this in a pejorative sense—a kind of political equivalent to Zeno's paradox.[10] Stanley Fish is playing with the political juxtaposition of static and dynamic frames. This is perhaps most evident in his construction of the search-for-truth rationale as an *inexorable semiotic deferral:* no matter how much progress is made in the search for truth, the target—the truth—can never be reached. The truth is always already receding from the advances that are made to reach it. That, of course, is because "the truth" has been constructed as a static object located in a future that is always already dynamically outdistancing our attempts to reach it. This sort of juxtaposition of static and dynamic frames may well be logically forbidden when dealing with motion in space, but politics is not logic. On the contrary, a good working definition of politics is: the art of the impossible.

Presented in this light, Stanley Fish's arguments above are all instantiations of a cardinal rule of politics: all politics worthy of the name presume, and indeed must presume, that the conditions they seek to realize are *already extant* to some significant degree. To what significant degree? The answer to that question depends, among other things, upon the content and configuration of the particular politics in question. This, of course, is something of a hedge.

So, to restate the point in an overly strong, but more interesting, fashion: any politics worthy of the name can only get started by presuming that its epistemics are in some significant way *already* in control, *already* in power. Now, to make that sort of presumption once one recognizes the historicity of one's own situation takes a lot of chutzpah. Historicity is what secures the contingency of epistemics. Historicity is what implies—no, it is what guarantees—the death of each and every politics and each and every epistemic (including each and every politics and every epistemic that seeks to become law). And so when chutzpah fails, what we have is dissonance—between what a politics holds to be necessary for its own realization and its perception of the field within which it is operating. This condition is hardly unique to contemporary liberalism. We can find utterly analogous instances in Marxism and in the other discursive offspring of the enlightenment.[11] The thing to recognize is that once this point is reached—once there is dissonance—the faith is shaken. It is at this point that a politics—any politics—becomes, in Stanley's Fish's words, "fraught with death." Fraught with intimations of its own death.

And it is precisely this loss of faith, this dissonance, that Fish describes and exploits so elegantly throughout his entire presentation. Indeed, if the partisans of the enlightenment liberal First Amendment seem so morose and so anguished, it is precisely because they cling to the necessity of drawing a certain set of iron-clad distinctions (the distinctions listed above) and yet recognize that not only does the world fail to conform to those distinctions, but that indeed, the world, as it is now, will never conform to those distinctions.

In short, what seems so disappointing to the First Amendment advocates in Fish's presentation is that free speech is impossible. Now, this notion that "free speech" is impossible seems like a startling conclusion until, of course, we remember that this was exactly the point with which Fish started his presentation. If you remember, he said right up front that free speech is impossible. He said, "There's no such thing as free speech."[12] And then he elaborated: speech is not free (1) because speech is constrained and constraining; (2) because (when it takes) it produces costs; and (3) because speech is not weightless. And then he said, "Free speech does not exist."[13] Now, if free speech is defined as a thing that does not exist, then it is a cinch that any view of the First Amendment which claims that its *raison d'être* is to protect free speech is at the very least somewhat confused. Indeed, in Fish's words, the First Amendment "will be protecting something that doesn't exist."[14] Yes, exactly so. Now, if the First Amendment has to go through Fish's text trying to protect something that doesn't exist, then it probably is not going to meet with a great deal of success.

Exactly so. And similarly, if the liberal enlightenment First Amendment with its strong objectivist cast has to defend itself in a world whose motions and movements are scripted by an animist like Fish (an animist who is keen on radical perspectivalism, suicidal conceptual purification, transitive conceptual contamination, and inexorable semiotic deferrals), then it's also a cinch that it won't last long. The game has been rigged at yet another level.

Indeed, Fish's argument has been totally and elegantly rigged—rigged through and through. Now, none of this is an objection to Stanley Fish's argument. Not at all. I realize that this may seem counterintuitive, so let me explain: If one were to say to someone like Ronald Dworkin that he has rigged the game, Dworkin would take that as an insult. But if one says this to Stanley Fish, he will take it as the highest form of compliment, because it is a confirmation of what he has been saying for some time now. Indeed, what he has been saying might be summarized in Lyotard's slogan, "Nothing can be said about reality that does not presuppose it." That is all there is. And for Stanley Fish, there is nothing to bemoan about this state of affairs.

One of the ironic twists here—one that may console the First Amendment advocates—is that most of what Stanley Fish is saying here actually has nothing to do in particular or in general with the First Amendment. *It has everything to do with the practices of fetishism and idolatry.* "The First Amendment," in Stanley Fish's essay, is the fetish—the main one of three—destined to take the fall. And if you remain fixated on "The First Amendment" you'll end up on the sidewalk, too, taking the fall as well. Now, you may think this is rather rude. But it's not. It's poetic justice: don't spend so much time looking at the cracks; watch where you are going. And another thing: learn to let go of your boxes ... even when they are marked with your favorite signifiers—signifiers like "The First Amendment."

Now, I grant you that as jurisprudential signifiers go, "The First Amendment" seems pretty powerful. In American jurisprudential cosmology, this "First Amendment" is no ordinary icon. But powerful as this signifier may be, it tends to pale next to the signifier marked "death." Take your time and think about it. If necessary, balance them for a while: on this side, "First Amendment"; on that side, "Death." "First Amendment"—"Death," "First Amendment"—"Death" O.K.?

Now, of course, Stanley Fish is not Ingmar Bergman, and law is not a chess game. But you had better believe that in Fish's argument, "Death" is going to win hands down against "The First Amendment." Indeed, he tells you so in his title: that "The First Amendment" is "Fraught with Death." Believe him. He really means it. Indeed, in all of Stanley Fish's essays (I may be overstating the point slightly) there is always a major signifier that some people usually care a great deal about that will take the hit—signifiers like "theory" or "critical self-consciousness" or "liberalism" and so on.[15]

Now here the main signifier fraught with death just happens to be the First Amendment. But there are two other signifiers also marked for death in Fish's essay: progressivism and skepticism. These, however, are lesser marks; they pale in the shadow of the signifier, "The First Amendment." Notice something about this signifier. In Stanley Fish's presentation, this signifier is fairly thin. Indeed, he says outright: it is "thin." And Fish also performatively demonstrates that it is thin. After all, what is this thing, "The First Amendment," in Stanley Fish's presentation? Well, for one thing, it is a self-consuming artifact: it is the kind of thing that keeps trying to protect something that doesn't exist—namely, free speech. Now, that is a really thin thing to do. But the signifier "The First Amendment" is thin in other ways as well: it is thin in the sense that in Fish's paper, "The First Amendment" is barely represented at all before it gets into serious trouble. In Fish's paper, that signifier, "The First Amendment," is fleshed out in only the sparsest manner—with a few quotes from distinguished law school professors and a few aphorisms from law's Nietzsche, Oliver Wendell Holmes (who, like the original, has already said everything worth saying).

This, then, is the identity of the First Amendment that bites the dust. No other. So if, like all these legal thinkers, you want to write on the body of *this* First Amendment, you have just made a serious category mistake. *This* First Amendment has no body. It is really thin. It is not worth writing on.

So if you actually cared when Fish's First Amendment bit the dust, then he got you. He got you, because there is no reason—a word that cannot possibly be used carefully enough here—to be at all upset when this essentially empty icon bites the dust. Fish's First Amendment is really thin. Not only does he tell you so— repeatedly—but performatively he keeps evacuating whatever content you might try to put in there. Why do you hang on? Or more precisely: just what is it that you are hanging on to?

So what is the point you say? What is Fish's message? Stanley Fish doesn't have a message. What he has is a rhetoric. Do you want to walk away with a message anyway? o.k. Here's a good one.[16] Do not take false gods. Do not worship graven images. Also, remember, Just do it. The alternative (and it is a bleak one), is that, as Stanley Fish puts it, "the condition of being a machine . . . may be the fate we make love to."[17]

And if you think this is too alarmist or too apocalyptic a vision even to consider, then I invite you to look at that other First Amendment—the one that is worked under by the Supreme Court of the United States of America. Think about that First Amendment. Indeed, consider that of all the excruciatingly over- wrought labyrinthine corridors of "The Constitution," it may be the First Amendment that is the most labyrinthine of them all. As rights go, the First Amendment is right up to date—it is bureaucracy made the best it can be. It is bureaucracy working itself pure—making itself into an endless subdivision of compart- ments each with its own test and its four-part or five-part very contextual factors. The United States Supreme Court and its academic groupies in the law schools have succeeded in doing what many, only a few decades ago, would have thought impossi- ble. They have succeeded in making Kafka look naive.

So there it is.

Is it possible after reading Fish to reconstruct a First Amendment that would be immune from these serious flaws? Sure, of course. Not to worry. But, remember—just as a cautionary suggestion—that it is also possible to reconstruct a unicorn. And note too that no matter how serious and rigorous your efforts at argumentative reconstruction of the unicorn may be, all you will have, at the end—assuming, of course, that things work out for the very best—is a "unicorn"—a "unicorn" preceded by very serious, very rigorous, supporting arguments.

IV

LAW WITHOUT END

EIGHT

Anti-Intellectualism

This is an essay about the genesis of anti-intellectualism within the American legal academy. The arguments and observations, however, have significance for other disciplines. Indeed, just as American law appropriates much from other disciplines, so do other academic disciplines appropriate much from American law.

To give but one example, the "rigor" claimed for analytical philosophy seems to be closely related to its attempt to emulate a juridical style, to construct law-like frames, law-like relations that are then used to adjudicate the validity of philosophical claims, in much the same way that a judge uses positive law to adjudicate the validity of various legal claims.

There is, indeed, a pervasive desire among many departments of the American university to establish formal disciplinary frames that enable academic claims to be produced, adjudicated, and, if appropriate, canonized. The desire to create such frames has something very law-like about it. And it is not hard to see what. Like law, such disciplines strive to legislate reality—*to create their own self-enclosing reality which can then be used to regulate and adjudicate the claims of others. Academic analytical philosophy is notorious for this sort of practice. But academic analytical philosophy is hardly alone in its imperial quest to lay down the law in "the contest of faculties." On the contrary, the juridical impulse runs deep and wide.*

The impulse to lay down the law is thus hardly limited to the legal academy. At the same time, that impulse is perhaps most obviously at home in this particular precinct of the University. And so it has been for a long time. Listen to the early dreams of law's empire. Listen to the words of the legal formalist, Joseph Beale:

> The teachers of law today have an increasing influence, and one which is comparable in degree with the part played by the judges, in the development of the law; and their power to mould professional opinion is likely to increase in the future more rapidly than that of the judges.
>
> —JOSEPH BEALE, *A Treatise on the Conflict of Laws* (1935)

There is a recurrent sameness to American legal thought. It is the sameness that comes from saying over and over again what the law is, and saying it, of course, in a way that conforms with the law itself.

But this is what American legal thinkers understand to be their role. Their role, as they understand it, is very much like the role of judges: it is emphatically to say what the law is.

And when American legal thinkers understand themselves to be authorized to say what the law is, it is not merely in a descriptive sense. Legal thinkers do not understand themselves merely to be astute observers of some practice called law; they understand themselves to be participants in the practice of law. They understand themselves authorized to say what law is in a prescriptive sense. In other words, they think that if their arguments are "good," if their reasoning is right, if their sources are correct, then their account of the law, their prescriptions, ought to be recognized by courts of competent jurisdiction. And the term "ought" here is not merely an external moral "ought," but an authoritative juridical ought: as they see it, their prescriptions ought to be followed as a matter of the internal requirements of law.

This rather pervasive attitude among legal thinkers is often *represented* as "the internal perspective"—namely, the perspective of a participant in the practice of law. Typically, the perspective of this participant is depicted as the perspective of the judge.[1]

As an intellectual matter, there are serious—quite possibly intractable—difficulties with this concept of "the internal perspective."[2] One of the great strengths, however, of the "internal perspective" is that it renders these difficulties imperceptible. Indeed, to the extent that one is already within the internal perspective, no questions seriously disruptive of the internal perspective can be asked. The reason is simple: the internal perspective rules out disruptive questions. This is not surprising. On the contrary, it is to be expected that any participant's perspective on his own practice will include the rhetorical means for the self-preservation of the practice. The "internal perspective" is an excellent rhetorical means. It serves at once as a theological guide for the faithful and as a disciplinary mechanism to police the boundaries of law's empire.

Among American legal thinkers, the internal perspective is a particularly persuasive device. Its persuasive force, as an intellectual re-presentation, stems precisely from its articulation of a primal and largely unnoticed self-identification of the legal thinker with the figure of the judge. It is this self-identification that leads American legal thinkers to consider law to be identical to "law" as it is re-presented from the perspective of the judge. Indeed, what American legal thinkers consider to be law is what the figure of the judge—a real judge, a sitting judge, a good judge, a smart judge, a politically enlightened judge, a composite judge—would consider to be "law."

The judge, accordingly, is not a monolithic figure—there are variations. And correspondingly, there are variations in what American legal thinkers consider "law." But it is the self-identification with the figure of the judge that establishes the pathways, limits, concerns, procedures, and preoccupations of American legal thinkers. Indeed, this self-identification of the legal academic with the subject-formation of the judge has been crucial to the construction of the "law" of the academy in several ways.

First, it is this self-identification that has enabled legal thinkers to construct and formalize something called "law" that, at the very least, simulates the appearance of an intellectual discipline. It is this identification that enables and sustains the fundamental formal ontology of law—the notion that law comes in object-forms such as rules, doctrines, principles, precedents, methods, models, theories, and so on. It is this identification as well that establishes what modes of "interpretation" or "reasoning" are deemed appropriate. In short, it is this self-identification that enables the tacit formalization of the field of law—a formalization that has itself served as the grounds for inquiry and disagreement by apologists and critics of law alike.

Second, it is this self-identification that establishes the intellectual orientation of American legal thinkers. Judges are supposed to produce decisions that maintain the rule of law, advance efficiency, keep the peace, produce justice, or achieve some such desired normative goal. In achieving these objectives, judges are supposed to show "good sense," "good judgment," or "reasonableness." In short, they are supposed to honor the norms, values, and beliefs that generally hold in the relevant authoritative community. The task of judges is very often to show that their judgment, opinion, or ruling is always already linked in some desired way with the best, the truest, the most faithful, the most progressive, the most lawful, the most [. . .] account of the relevant authoritative community's norms, values, and beliefs. In their self-identification with judges, legal thinkers take on the same orientation. The result is that intellectual inquiry is subordinated to and guided by normative starting points, channels, and end-goals that are presumed to hold within the relevant authoritative community. Now, of course, a great deal of American legal thought is quite "critical" in tone—aimed at criticizing specific opinions, doctrines, statutory schemes, methods, theories, and so on. But it is important to remember that this criticism occurs along very narrow lines and that the vast majority of this criticism does not trouble the fundamental ontological forms, the formal order, or the desirable eschatology widely assumed to underlie American law.

Third, this self-identification with the subject-formation of the judge establishes a set of intellectual tasks for legal academics — namely, the tracing of law back through its authoritative materials, the policing and normalization of new forms of legal thought, the recognition and conceptualization of new juridical problems, the expulsion of spurious or subversive jurisprudential tendencies, and the perfection and general improvement of existing formulations of law. All this is done, of course, in the idioms, within the forms of reasoning and interpretation practiced by judges. Indeed, the *pièce de resistance* in the academy (the law review article) is a morphological mimesis of the legal brief, of the bench memo. Even where the substance of this *pièce de resistance* may seem far removed from traditional legal concerns or traditional legal materials, its "form" will bear an uncanny resemblance to the aesthetics of the legal brief, the bench memo, and, ultimately, the opinion. Hence, even when legal thinkers leave the realm of addressing sitting or imaginary judges, to do theory, to address legislatures, or to engage in "politics," their thought remains very much within the aesthetic frames and the normative orientations characteristic of addressing sitting or imaginary judges. It is true that the academic production may be expected to show a higher degree of reflexivity, or self-consciousness, than its juridical counterpart, but not so much as to actually pose a serious threat to the fundamental ontological forms, the formal order, and the desirable eschatology always already assumed to underwrite American law.

Yet in some ways, the self-identification of the legal thinker with the figure of the judge is wearing thin. It is becoming somewhat abstract. And it is fragmenting as well. Indeed, as legal thinkers take intellectual, aesthetic, or political distance from the present work product of the courts, the image of the judge with which they identify becomes increasingly removed from the possible identities of sitting judges. And for some legal thinkers, their self-identification becomes, as a matter of substance, more beholden to client-groups or political causes than to the figure of the judge. In these ways, the self-identification of legal thinkers with the figure of the judge seems to be disintegrating. The appellate judge is losing intellectual status as the central organizing subject formation of American legal thought. But even as the self-identification of legal thinkers with the figure of the judge is becoming increasingly strained and increasingly improbable, legal thinkers are still living its history. The self-identification survives at an abstract, but nonetheless foundational, level. It survives as an aesthetic, in the fundamental ontological forms and in the pervasive normative orientation of American legal thought.

Unfortunately, the self-identification of the legal thinker with the figure of the judge has certain fatal implications. That is because the world of the judge is one whose contours and content are structured to produce satisfactory judicial resolutions. The judge has tasks to perform. His categories, idioms, and perspectives are shaped by those tasks. The production of knowledge, the acquisition of insight, the achievement of intellectual edification are not high on his agenda. His categories, idioms, and perspectives are (quite understandably) aimed resolutely at closure, at resolution. And perhaps that is even the way it should be. But legal academics are not judges. Legal academics have neither the responsibility, nor the competence, nor the grounding context of real stakes to allow them to be judges. When legal academics take on the persona of the judge, they become pretend-judges issuing pretend-law. And no matter how sincerely and authentically this role is assumed, the fact remains that the legal academic will be writing a law review article, not a judicial opinion—with all the differences implied in the different social meanings of these two artifacts.

Ironically, the self-identification of the legal academic with the judge is never complete—it always remains imperfect. And every legal academic knows this. Not a one dares to close an article with the line at which the supporting legal argument quite self-evidently aims: "It is so ordered." But while the self-identification is never perfect—always residually inauthentic, always a kind of failed simulation—there is nonetheless much that is sacrificed in this self-identification. This self-identification with the figure of the judge has resulted in producing a law of the academy with certain pervasive intellectual deficits. I will mention two here. The first is the *radical simplification of law.* The second is *the juridification of legal thought.*

The self-identification of the legal thinker with the judge reduces various interactions among different subject formations—lawyers, clients, judges, citizens, witnesses, experts, and so on—to the perspective of one actor, the judge. This singular perspective is then simply assumed to be regulative of all that might be considered "law." This identification with the subject-formation of the judge produces the (relative) singularity of perspective that allows all that might be called "law" to precipitate and crystallize into a (seemingly) stabilized ontology of "rules," "doctrines," "principles," "methods," and so on that seem verily as if they exist independently of any subject. It is the legal academic's identification with the subject-formation of the judge that produces the belief that these object-forms (rules, doctrines, principles, methods) have an existence independent of any subject's beliefs. It is, in short, this identification and the resulting limited perspective of the judge that yields the usual pre-critical positing of fundamental ontological forms that thereby enable most of what American legal thinkers call "law" to even occur.

The identity of this one actor—the judge—is typically such

that he or she is presumed to have tremendous (even if typically undetermined) power to declare what relations will regulate the behavior of the other actors. The judge, in the courtroom as on the law teacher's blackboard, occupies a superior, an elevated position—as if he or she were somehow above the other actors, ontologically endowed with a great power over the actions of the others.

To identify with the figure of the judge yields a kind of *double incapacitation.* In one sense, the identification with the judge truncates the perspectival possibilities to a singular perspective and thus misses *ab initio* much of what is interesting (and problematic) about law—namely, its genesis from the different perceptions, actions, and re-presentations of various different actors: judges, lawyers, clients, witnesses, press, and so on. To enshrine oneself in the position of the judge is to miss almost entirely the processes of juris-genesis—the processes by which law comes to be formed as law. It is to assume into existence an entire juridical world of artifacts like "rules" and "doctrines" and "principles" and "methods," whose identities are not only already ontologically secure, but are, supposedly, already ruling, already "in force," as it were. In short, the self-identification with the judge assumes away much of what is interesting and mysterious about law.

The identification with the figure of the judge is incapacitating in another sense. In addition to its blinding effect, it also produces a sense of false empowerment. The judge is a figure who believes *ab initio,* as a matter of social aesthetics, in the efficacy of law. This is someone who believes, as a matter of course, that "law" has certain obvious and nonproblematic regulative relations to its field of application—relations that bear names like "deterrence" or "facilitation." This is someone who is given to believing fairly frequently, and often rather improbably so, that because the law decrees something, it will in fact be so. This is someone who believes that juridical concepts like specific intent or linear causation or individual autonomy are valid, not merely as juridical concepts, but as descriptions of social life. Indeed, the self-identification of the legal thinker with the figure of the judge yields the belief that juridical concepts—concepts such as consent, coercion, public, individual, and so on—actually map onto the social world in relatively obvious, nonproblematic ways. The self-identification with the figure of the judge thus precludes any critical appreciation of the character or identity of the categories and relations of law. And it is precisely the resulting false empowerment that leads legal thinkers to have wildly utopian assessments about the normative consequences of their own legal thought and law in general.

The self-identification with the figure of the judge is precisely what leads legal thinkers to believe that they are not only studying law, but that they are in fact "doing" law. It is indeed this conceit that underwrites the otherwise rather odd, though widespread, belief among American legal thinkers that *prescribing* solutions, methods, or even attitudes is somehow a useful or effective way to alter the behavior of legal actors—most particularly, judges. This belief in the effectiveness of normative *prescription* among legal thinkers is an unconscious mimesis of the judge's belief in the effectiveness of judicial orders. The judge concludes the opinion with the phrase, "It is so ordered." The legal thinker imitates the gesture by concluding the scholarly work with "And therefore, the court should . . . ." Or, "We should . . . ." Or, "Somebody should . . . ."

It is in such ways that *the radical simplification of law* is achieved.

The self-identification of legal thinkers with the figure of the judge also yields what might be called *the juridification of legal thought*. It is through this self-identification that all manner of habits, rhetorics, even forms of social organization proper to judges become part of American legal thought. The intellectual vehicle for this transposition is the internal perspective. But again, it is the implicit self-identification of the legal thinker with the judge that produces the results—many of which are radically anti-intellectual.

As one example, the self-identification of legal thinkers with judges enables legal thinkers to rule from the bench. Hence, legal thinkers routinely dismiss entire forms of thought as if they were dismissing an appeal, as if they were rejecting an appellate argument. There are numerous examples of this practice.[3] Over time, this tendency of American legal thought to receive intellectual currents through the adjudicatory medium and judicial habits of thought is not only anti-intellectual but self-destructive. Indeed, if legal thinkers systematically fail to deal *seriously* with new intellectual currents, then it cannot be expected that the law of the academy will learn much of anything new. Nor can it be expected that it will remain vital. On the contrary, this arrogation of the imperial rhetoric of the appellate judge so as to rule from the bench on the value of intellectual currents precludes engagement. Ultimately, what this habit of thought can be counted on to produce is a law that is in a state of arrested development—a law incapable of learning anything new, incapable of generating new inquiries or new insights, a law that cannot do anything except reaffirm itself as always already the same, even as it crafts new names for itself.

This is arguably the state of the legal academy at present. What is produced by and large today is a law that reinvents itself as always already the same (only different). This may sound like a disturbingly impossible enterprise. In folk culture, it is called, "reinventing the wheel." In the literature of classical Greece, it is called the Myth of Sisyphus. In law, it bears a much more respectable name—in fact, quite a popular name. The name is "reconstruction" and it is generally considered a good thing. Indeed, legal thinkers are forever striving to reconstruct this or that—everything from promissory estoppel to the law of gender. "Reconstruction," of course, is what legal thinkers want most for their law. What they want—in accordance with the authoritative character of law—is to construct, to create a law that is itself already law. They want a law that is at once the same as the old law and yet different. The reconstructed "law" has to be the same as the old law so that it can in fact be law, as opposed to wishful thinking. But it also has to be different from the old law so that it can avoid the manifest defects of the old law. Reconstruction is the polite term used to identify this quixotic enterprise.

Another aspect of the juridification of legal thought lies in the subordination of inquiry to normative commitments associated with or at least compatible with the rule of law. Normative commitments define the starting points, the frame, and the permissible end points of legal thought. Thus, if a line of intellectual inquiry poses a threat to "law" or to its fundamental normative commitments, then the line of inquiry is susceptible to being called "nihilistic." The further implication is that therefore the line of inquiry should not be pursued. The upshot is that if one is engaged in legal thought, one is obliged to re-present the practice of "law," however degraded its actual condition may be, as nonetheless *essentially* justified, coherent, rational, and good. Not only is this orientation profoundly anti-intellectual, but, indeed, it is the mark of a degenerative enterprise—one that prefers its pleasing baubles of moralistic self-congratulation to any serious reckoning with its own identity and actions. One suspects that phrenologists, too, must once have been quite opposed to the "corrosive" character of "critical" thought.[4]

Another aspect of the juridification of legal thought is the aesthetic subordination of intellectual and cultural insights. Indeed, before they gain admission to law's empire, intellectual and cultural insights from other disciplines must be recast in the forms and the uses that accord with the aesthetics of the law of the judge: the legal brief, the bench memo. It is in this way that deconstruction is reduced to a legal reasoning *technique*, that hermeneutics is crystallized into a *method* for advancing progressive legal thought.[5] It is in this way that [. . .] is degraded into [. . .]. To the extent that those who do law in the academy constantly degrade intellectual insight and resources by transforming them into "legal authorities," "methods," "techniques," and the like, they are destroying cognitive capacity. They are homogenizing the "internal perspective" and depleting its repertoires of possibility. This erasure of perspective, this collapse of opposition, this destruction of scale produces an intellectually flattened legal universe—"the night in which, as we say, all cows are black."[6]

Still another aspect of the juridification of legal thought is the reliance on "magic words." Students, during their first year of law school, learn that in some legal contexts certain words are magic, in that their mere invocation can be guaranteed to induce certain effects upon legal actors. Such words might include "notice," or "possession," or "strict scrutiny." Legal thinkers often exhibit a haughty derision for the magic words—treating them as unfortunate (though perhaps necessary) legacies of an old and much reviled legal formalism. Nonetheless, contemporary legal thinkers clearly have their own set of magic words—words like "values" and "rights" and "reason."[7] These are words which, when uttered in appropriate grammatical sentences, can be counted upon to reduce even the most powerful legal minds to displays of respectful worship or docile submission.

Of all such magic words, "reason" may well be the one that commands the most universal assent. As in various kinds of earlier shamanistic practices, legal thinkers will often repeat the terms "reason" or "reasonableness" over and over again as if the mere repetition of the terms will make reason and reasonableness themselves appear.[8] This is the same rather bizarre, though widespread, confusion that enables legal thinkers to believe that in virtue of *advocating* reason, goodness, or moral wonderfulness, they are themselves engaged in an enterprise that is reasoned, good, or morally wonderful. At the limit, it is this confusion that enables them to believe that, in virtue of their *advocacy* of reason, goodness, or moral wonderfulness, they are themselves reasoned, good, or morally wonderful. This kind of immensely self-flattering belief is quite widespread among legal thinkers. It is also a non sequitur.

But these are all small-scale examples of the anti-intellectual implications of the legal thinker's self-identification with the figure of the judge. The more serious implication is a large-scale one. The identification with the figure of the judge is an intellectual betrayal. It is an intellectual betrayal because, in important ways, the judge cannot speak the truth, must routinely dissemble, has, in fact taken oaths that require subordination of truth, understanding, and insight, to the preservation of certain bureaucratic governmental institutions and certain sacred texts. To be self-identified with the subject formation of the judge is thus to be intellectually compromised. It is to be beholden to a rhetoric, an aesthetic, and normative commitments that are pervasively anti-intellectual—that are, in fact, destructive of intellectual endeavor.[9]

Sadly, the legal thinkers of many generations have had to labor under the signs of a law that confused and conflated advocacy with scholarship.[10] For perhaps a very few—those who sought and obtained appointment to this or that court or agency—this may have been a successful enterprise. But for all the others, they compromised intellectual possibility to exercise a shadow juridical power—a power they manifestly never had. A few were judges in waiting. Some were appointed. Most waited. As for the rest, it must have been one very long session of moot court.

NINE

1. *The*
2. *Legal*
3. *Form*
4. *of*
5. *Being*

The first year [of law school] aims to drill into you the more essential techniques of handling cases. The hardest job of the first year is to lop off your common sense, to knock your ethics into temporary anesthesia. Your view of social policy, your sense of justice—to knock these out of you along with woozy thinking, along with ideas all fuzzed around the edges. You are to acquire the ability to think precisely, to analyze coldly, to work within a body of materials that is given, to see, and see only, and manipulate, the machinery of the law.

—*Karl Llewellyn, The Bramble Bush* (1930)

For those who are legally trained, the violence of the law is extremely difficult to recall. It is difficult to recall because even where it emerges it does so in a legitimated form. The violence of law emerges everywhere under the guise of the already authorized or under the guise of the necessarily justified.[1] For those who are legally trained, the question of law's violence is immediately apprehended within a normative orientation that transforms the enterprise of recollection into a normative question of whether this violence is authorized or justified, how or when it can be authorized or justified (and so on).

Nonetheless, there is a limited (and opposed) sense in which it is easy to recognize this violence. It is easy because this violence is inscribed everywhere. One can begin, then, by recognizing the violence of the law in its obvious manifestations: the violent outcomes of judicial decisions—the compelled transfers of wealth, the forced incarcerations, the death sentences signaled by the last line of the opinion which reads, "It is so ordered." This violence of law is inscribed throughout legal proceedings which at all points authoritatively delimit, shape, and compel what is said and what is done. Indeed, in the very idea of law there is, of course, a necessary, a law-constituting violence—the violence of reductionism, the violence of nonrecognition, the violence of exclusion, and the violence of compulsory performance. The important point here is that this violence is an inexorable ontological aspect of a law that claims to be *authoritative*.

For those who must administer and practice this law, this violence must be kept contained and repressed.[2] This is in part why judicial opinions, legal briefs, and courtroom procedures have such a formalized character. Everyone associated with the administration of this law is in virtue of the stylized courtroom choreography, the depersonalized power-clothing, the stilted specialized language, the immaculate typo-free papers, at once distanced from the violence and authorized to visit this violence on witnesses, clients, and so on.

This repressed violence is the manifestation of a deeper, more profound violence. It is a violence that Nietzsche describes in the "Genealogy of Morals," where he writes of how conscience, responsibility, duty, and guilt come into the world. For Nietzsche, they come into the world as man becomes capable of making promises. Constructing a being capable of promises is no simple matter. Nietzsche writes:

But how many things this presupposes. To ordain the future in advance in this way, man must first have learned to distinguish necessary events from chance ones, to think causally, to see and anticipate distant eventualities as if they belonged to the present, to decide with certainty what is the goal and the means to it, and in general be able to calculate and compute. Man himself must first of all have become *calculable, regular, necessary, even in his own image of himself* if he is to be able to stand security for his own future which is what one who promises does.[3]

How did man come to be calculable, regular, necessary? How did he come to remember his promises? It was through law—a law that burned its requirements into memory:

> Consider the old German punishments; for example stoning (the sagas already have millstones drop on the head of the guilty), breaking on the wheel (the most characteristic invention and speciality of the German genius in the realm of punishment!) piercing with stakes, tearing apart or trampling by horses ("quartering"), boiling of the criminal in oil or wine (still employed in the fourteenth and fifteenth centuries), the popular flaying alive ("cutting straps"), cutting flesh from the chest, and also the practice of smearing the wrongdoer with honey and leaving him in the blazing sun for the flies.[4]

It is through "the aid of such images and procedures," Nietzsche says, that "one finally remembers five or six 'I will not's' in regard to which one has given one's promise so as to participate in the advantages of society."[5]

In Nietzsche's genealogy, the violent origins of the law as well as morality are thus revealed. These violent origins are not surpassed. They endure.[6] They endure first as a cultural form that must be assumed, as a legacy that must be lived. For Nietzsche, there is something gained: what is gained is law—namely, "a means of putting an end to the senseless raging of *ressentiment*."[7] Nietzsche is no one-sided critic of the law. But for Nietzsche, there is something lost as well. What has been lost is that man has made himself "calculable, regular, necessary."

In law, in legal argument, in law school, in legal opinions, in law review articles, there is virtually never any reckoning of what has been lost. There is only the unrestrained celebration of what has been gained. In law, what we have are one-sided worshipers—worshipers who in their passion to celebrate law are driven to increasingly improbable descriptions of the law.

Here, we will consider what has been lost.

To say that man must make himself "calculable, regular, necessary" is to say that, in each succeeding generation, each human being must somehow become a fit subject of law. Each must somehow assume in court, in the deposition room, and in everyday life the aesthetic of law's designated subjects—the free-willed individual, the reasonable person, the person in good faith, and so on. At an obvious and trivial level, this entails complying with the substantive requirements of law. Much more significantly, this entails assuming the formal aesthetic of the subjects established by law and traveling the regulatory channels marked out for those subjects.

In our age, of course, this means making oneself into a kind of bureaucratic subject—with all the compartmentalization, the specialization, the layered hierarchies of expertise-knowledge forms that this entails. To be a fit subject of law in our age is in effect to be a bureaucrat—to pay one's bills on time, to manage one's money, to buy insurance, to comply with various paper production requirements of various government agencies, one's own employer, and one's patrons.

This brings us to a second way in which the violent origins of law endure. They endure as an ongoing *intensification of subjection* to legal process. At the political level, this ongoing subjection is marked by the transition from the liberal democratic state to the administrative welfare state. This is the transition in which the boundary between the political state and civil society, between public and private is erased.

With this erasure, legal process is extended in a way that subsumes more and more aspects (even trivial aspects) of existence to law's dominion and control. To every problem there is a solution—and the solution is almost always some version of "there ought to be a law." Not only does the positive law proliferate in many layers of self-referential commands, directives, exceptions, and limitations, but indeed legalism becomes the dominant mode of social and cognitive organization. Legalism defines the internal institutional configurations of HMOs, corporations, the family, social clubs, homeowners' associations, universities.

And it is easy to see how the extension of legal process occurs. Consider three related forms of extension: *strategic compliance, strategic self-representation,* and *simulation and emulation.*

In one sense, the law's dominion and control is extended through a process of *strategic compliance.* This entails both the conscious and unconscious inscription of law's metaphors, categories and concepts within the institutions and within the agents subject to law. For instance, once a corporation becomes subject to a legal decree, its lawyers respond by trying to organize the corporation to comply with the decree and to avoid manufacturing evidence of any further violation. The corporation through its various agents establishes corporate policy and compliance procedures to enforce those policies. The various departments are advised. Agents within the corporation are named and designated to monitor the policies. Formal communication channels are authorized. Compliance documents are created. Legal realities are established through exchanges of communications. Violations of the procedures are penalized. In this way, mere compliance with the law entails restructuring institutional and human subjects in forms, in aesthetics, to which the law will attach a desirable (as opposed to undesirable) recognition. Almost always, it is necessary to offer up to the law a subject formation, an action pattern, that it already understands and will thus recognize.[8]

Now, in turn, as social institutions organize themselves in legal metaphors, categories and concepts, these become inscribed in professional idioms, in cognitive schemes, in the very ways in which human beings frame their world.

In a second sense, the extension of legal process occurs through the formation of interest groups seeking legislative, administrative, or juridical existence, recognition, and beneficence. This might be called *strategic self-representation*. Indeed, social and economic existence, for many, depends upon achieving the status of beneficiary—beneficiary of legislative, administrative, or juridical largesse.[9] In the administrative welfare state, all kinds of groups and individuals strive (consciously or not) to represent and organize themselves as jural ontological identities deserving of government largesse. Economic opportunities for many professionals (appraisers, social workers, engineers, and so on) depend significantly on securing part of a legislatively, judicially, or administratively defined market as consultants, certifiers, or the like. The result, of course, is that these groups and their members organize and represent themselves (as well as their knowledges) in a legalistic aesthetic. *To be in America is to be a function of a legal subject.*

All sorts of different groups seem to know this. Hence, one of the primary ways that social clubs, homeowners' associations, collectives, and cooperatives secure their own institutional existence is through the adoption of constitutions, bylaws, and even the adoption of Roberts' rules of order. In doing this, they are engaged in a process of *simulation and emulation*. They are simulating and emulating *the legal form of being*. This is understandable. Law being one of the primary forms of political legitimation in American culture, jural form becomes an aesthetic of legitimation for all manner of social groups and institutions. Law becomes an aesthetic of legitimation not just in a moralistic sense but in an ontological sense as well. Legalism becomes a kind of social ontology; It becomes the very organizational structure, the very medium of self-constitution of various social groups.

In all these ways, human beings must conform their behavior and their minds to a legalistic aesthetic. In order for all this law to be maintained and reproduced, all its considerable violence — everything from the obvious violence of litigation outcomes to the much more subtle but pervasive violence of bureaucratic proliferation — must be eclipsed. In particular, it must be eclipsed from those subjects who are most intimately involved in the production of this violence. It must, in short, be eclipsed from the judge, the lawyer, the law student, and the legal academic. This eclipsing is itself achieved through the related processes of legitimation and subject formation.

Legitimation first. Many of the legitimations of the law are themselves contained within its various canonical texts — the cases, the statutes, the constitution, and so on. These materials contain all manner of what might be called legitimation complexes — complexes that serve to authorize and justify the violence of law. There are various complexes. Here is a sketch of a few:

Equivalency Complexes

Many of these legitimation complexes work by establishing some sort of equivalency between a party's actions and the judge's order. For instance, the ascription of mental states (intention, recklessness, negligence) serves as a kind of equivalency rating. Linear conceptions of causation are also used throughout American law to establish equivalencies between harm and remedy.

The appeal of the equivalency complexes is that it appears as if the judge or the decision maker contributes nothing to the decision except to ensure that the equivalencies are properly observed. The action of the judge appears merely as a correction of a momentary imbalance in the previously established order.

Consent Complexes

Many of the justification complexes work in such a way as to allow ascription of consent (hence, self-rule) to the party sanctioned by the law. These complexes do their work by attributing present legal decisions to the agency of an animistic, normatively pleasing supra-individual subject formation—anything from "reason," "the rule of law," "we the people," to "the founding fathers," or the like.

Hence it is that the work product of nine rather harried bureaucrats on Capitol Hill in Washington, D.C., are routinely represented as the Constitutional decisions of the founding fathers, or even more grandly as decisions of "We the people . . ." Sometimes even more transparently animistic practices are brought into play, as when judges say that "the rule of law is binding . . ." or when they say, "The Constitution requires. . . ."[10] Indeed, any number of metaphysically and normatively comforting supra-individual subject-formations are invoked so that the violence of the law is always already represented as duly authorized.

The consent complex works by forging an identification between the citizen or the individual, who is himself cast as an autonomous coherent free-willed subject, with such animistic normatively pleasing supra-individual subject formations. The free-willed subject here is the subject formation enacted by the party who is going to be visited with a fortunate (or unfortunate) legal consequence. He is the one who is going to learn very soon that he has just "chosen" or "accepted" or "waived" something.

Hierarchy Complexes

Many of the legitimation complexes of law are structured in the form of hierarchies of consideration. These complexes include obvious formally recognized hierarchies (i.e., source of law arguments: the Constitution trumps statutory law trumps common law) as well as formally unrecognized hierarchies (i.e., the exact reverse: statutes as interpreted against a background of common law, the Constitution as interpreted as against a background of statutes). Less obviously, these hierarchies include the countless, much more context-specific forms of reasoning that constitute the "professional knowledge" of lawyers and that remain largely inaccessible (and perhaps incomprehensible) to the lay public.

Teleological Complexes

Much of American law is cast on the image of progress—of law as progressing inexorably in a favorable direction. Hence, laws are commonly assumed to have purposes or objectives that can in fact be reached. And a great deal of contemporary legal thought is of this teleological character—prescribing norms to achieve efficiency, to fulfill policy objectives, to maximize utility, to help a victim group, to advance certain values or goals, to achieve liberation, to make law the best it can be (and so on).

These teleological complexes are increasingly popular in the legal academy and in the courts. The obvious appeal of this kind of reasoning is its extraordinary relaxation of constraints. This kind of teleological thought is notoriously indiscriminate in allowing any action to seem good (or bad) or worthwhile (or worthless). Within the teleological aesthetic, virtually nothing can be falsified. A glorious and unverifiable future is thus used to validate present pain.

These legitimation complexes, of course, cannot and do not stand alone. They are enabled and sustained by a crucial formative identification in which the legal actor or legal thinker is prompted to identify with the figure of the judge. This formative identification is instilled in the student. Among legal academics (and, of course, judges) this identification is at once lasting and pervasive. Among lawyers, the identification tends to break down somewhat.[11]

The judge is the figure in American law whose perspective, interests, and concerns delimit and stabilize what is called "law." Since the time of Langdell at least (and still today), it is the judge's work-product, the judicial opinion, that constitutes the vast bulk of materials for three years of law school. The judicial opinion and the judicial persona provide the implicit framing and orientation for the presentation and elaboration of the "law" of the academy. The legal academic identifies strongly with the judge. This identification is largely the result of having played the part of the judge as a student—having had to answer questions such as, "What would you do?" "How would you decide?" For the legal academic this identification with the judge is even further reinforced through the mentoring ritual of the judicial clerkship—a rite of passage that was long considered crucial for obtaining an academic appointment at elite legal institutions.

Unlike the judge, the academic cannot conclude his writings, his thoughts, with the authority of "It is so ordered." But in the legal academy, the judge's "It is so ordered" is expressed in the formally symmetrical "And therefore, the court should . . ." or the more abstract "We should . . ." or yet again "Somebody else should . . . ." The legal academic likes to fancy himself as a judge of the judges.

Now, this identification of the legal academic and the law student with the judge masks a certain violence. Simply by taking on the tasks, perspectives, orientations, and idioms of the judge, the violence of the law becomes obscured. And that is because the judge is himself a figure of violence—one who, to perform his task, cannot take serious cognizance of this violence.

It is he who presides over the violence of the courtroom. It is he who is constantly seeking to impose the template of "the law" on situations whose meanings exceed any template. The judge is thus always involved in this reductionist enterprise. Even when he seeks out information, dialogue, context, understanding (and so on), it is always a search that remains subordinate to the task of achieving that monistic resolution. (It is so ordered.)

Because the role of the judge institutes such a normative premium upon satisfactory resolution, judges must begin with starting points that enable resolution. This means they must remain blind to the violence in which they engage. Indeed, if judges could see the violence of their enterprise, it may be doubted that they would be able to perform their judicial function very well. Indeed, if the law routinely enabled serious recognition of its own violence, it is only those with a taste for violence who would be attracted to judging. And, of course, given such tastes, it may be doubted that they would make appealing judges.

But it is not only recognition of their own violence that judges must eschew. They must also avoid taking cognizance of any social, psychological, anthropological knowledge or insight that would prevent a normatively satisfactory juridical resolution. The net effect of this rhetorical economy of the judicial opinion is that *the ontology of law is dictated by its normative needs. Or to put it plainly: in law something does or does not exist depending on whether it has a favorable or a nonfavorable normative implications for the continued practice of law.* In the rhetorical space between its ontological premises and its normative conclusions, the judicial opinion is a rather small, indeed crimped, intellectual universe.

It turns out then that the judge is a figure whose intellectual universe is necessarily narrow, a figure whose intellectual capacity is severely limited, a figure, in short, who in order to do his job *"wants very much not to see, wants not to understand, wants not to pursue certain lines of inquiry."* [12] This is why judicial opinions are, as Richard Posner says, "mediocre texts."

But not only are these texts, these judicial opinions, intellectually impoverished artifacts; they are ethically deceitful as well. They are deceitful in the sense that their normative requirements require the logic of misrepresentation. Hence, despite the fact that law is quite obviously a rich amalgamation of feudal social aesthetics, nineteenth-century juristic science, early twentieth century legal realist policy analysis, legal process proceduralisms, Warren Court normativity, judicial opinions routinely strive to represent this dissonant mélange as if it were coherent and sensible.

Imagine that for a three-year period you had to read thousands of these mediocre texts. Imagine further that you had to show up in the morning every weekday and answer excruciatingly specific questions on the details of these texts. Imagine, in other words, that you had to be a law student.

The combination of reading mediocre texts and having to pay great attention to the details of these mediocre texts is not the sort of sustained exercise that can be expected to produce great minds. On the contrary, after three years of continuous administration it can produce certain cognitive deficits. And indeed, the people who undergo this process have a very hard time breaking out of the narrow aesthetic channels that have been cognitively inscribed.

While these texts called judicial opinions basically rehearse the same rather simple legitimation complexes and the same recurrent set of distinctions—private/public, free will/coercion, etc.— rarely is this formative aesthetic revealed to the student. Rather, this crucial formative aesthetic is imparted to the student *sub rosa* through a process of unreflective exposure in the case law, and through the repetition of a patterned set of questions. These questions often seem piercingly specific to a case, but in fact they very often tend to repeat the relatively simple aesthetic structure of American law.[13]

This process is mind-numbing in itself, because what is never questioned, what, indeed, cannot be seriously questioned (for there is no disciplinary knowledge base and no method in law to question it) are the questions themselves. It is in this way, that the questions (not being questioned themselves) become, unreflectively, part of the student's unconscious aesthetic pre-figuration of law (and the student's pre-figuration of social life).

And, of course, as one might imagine, the more cases one reads, the more mind-numbing this process becomes. At the level of the individual who undergoes this experience, this is a tragic process. After all, law school advertises itself as training people to think very hard, very critically.

But what actually occurs in law school is on a different order. What one learns in law school is to think very hard, very critically within a narrowly channeled social and legal aesthetic—an aesthetic that remains itself unquestioned and that ultimately becomes imprinted as the repertoire of cognitive possibility in the mind of the law student, the law student to become lawyer, the law student to become law teacher.[14]

How is it that virtually no one notices this? Law has two advantages in this respect. The first advantage is that law as a discipline is not subject to any sort of verification procedure whatsoever. Cases end whenever the appellate process comes to an end. The last opinion by the highest authorized court is what counts. After that, the judge, the legal academic, the law student typically move on to the next case. Correspondingly, the case, the analysis, the class discussion ends with an opinion. "It is so ordered." "The court should . . . ." "We should . . . ."

The second advantage is that for many of the law students, their first introduction to the social field ostensibly regulated by law is the law itself. Many law students' first understanding of the business world, of mergers, buy-outs, debentures, stocks, commercial paper, contracts, or anything of the sort is through the lens of the law itself. Hence, for instance, the law student's understanding of how contracts work (or don't work) is framed through the prisms of contract doctrine. The result, of course, is that between contract law and the objects it ostensibly regulates, there is an almost magical perfect fit. And when the fit is not perfect, it is, of course, because the disputing parties have inexplicably failed to follow the law. When students learn legal doctrine, they learn it twice, in a double gesture. They learn legal doctrine as the law. And they learn legal doctrine as social theory.

Now it becomes possible to understand how the violence of the law is eclipsed. The violence that the law directs outward on others is a violence that it practices internally upon itself and upon the subjects called upon to do its work.

V

EPILOGUE

TEN

Laying Down the Law

For American legal thinkers, the focus of legal thought is always either law's relation to its own internal requirements (formalism) or law's relation to its object (legal realism). These are the two great moments of American law. A great deal of legal argument consists largely of preferring (or arguing for) one moment or the other. A great deal of legal argument also consists in fleshing out what these relations mean.

But, of course, there is a third relation—one that is almost never mentioned in American law. This third relation is one between law and the subjects who invoke its name. To understand law, one must appreciate and understand the identity of the subjects who invoke its name, for the identity of the law that is invoked will have a great deal to do with their interests, desires, aesthetics, needs (and so on).

Given the peculiar aesthetics and ideology of American law, this third relation, the relation of law to the subject, has not been a focal point of interest in the legal academy or anywhere else. Legal academics, judges, lawyers, law students are simply not accustomed to understanding what they treat as "law" as a product of their own interests, desires, aesthetics, needs (and so on).

This failure is, I would argue, essential to the production of what we conceive as "law" in the first place. To put it another way, this failure is indispensable to the constitution of this thing we call "law." The law's identity as autonomous, neutral, objective, stabilized—and so on depends upon this failure of recognition. This is not semantic imperialism on my part. I have no wish to define "law." This is simply a general observation of what American legal professionals as well as the lay public take to be, recognize as, and respond to as "law."

The point may be wrong. But if it is right—and, of course, that is a matter of more or less, not yes or no—then the constitution of law as this failure of self-recognition also succeeds in producing an always and already defective law—a law that is always something less than what it is claimed to be.

For instance, what legal academics call "law" is often largely a product of their academic circumstances—the need to produce intellectually respectable tracts. More fundamentally it is in part a product of the academics' needs to represent themselves as "knowing" something, to represent themselves as possessed of a discipline. What judges call "law" may be a product of the ethically taxing circumstances in which they work. It may also be a product of a felt need to clear their dockets. What law students call "law" may be a function of their need to believe that they are actually learning something of enduring value.

My view—one which has been explored throughout these essays—is that the failure to consider this third relation, this problem of the subject, has led to serious deficiencies in American law. It has led to the inscription of all sorts of intellectually, aesthetically, and ethically objectionable practices in law. Specifically, what American legal actors and legal thinkers have treated as law includes various forms of mysticism and fetishism.

Compounding these unfortunate legal inscriptions is that American legal thinkers have nonetheless sought all along to represent this mysticism, and fetishism, as rational and good.

This belief that law is itself good is a category mistake that has afflicted the last two or three generations of legal academics.

(More generations, actually. But, here I will only mention the recent past.) These generations have all wanted, for their peculiar generational reasons, to think really well of law. First, there was *the legal process generation* which saw in law the possibilities of perfecting order and procedural regularity through careful craftsmanship. This was the generation that wanted to think well of law because somehow it saw "the rule of law" as a bulwark against totalitarian regimes. As others have observed, this generation saw in law something good which the U.S. clearly had and the Communists clearly did not. Following on the heels of the legal process generation was *the Warren Court generation*. This was the generation that saw "law" as a tool for the realization of liberal philosophy's idea of justice. With the Warren Court sitting, this generation thought well of law because it saw the courts as agencies of progressive social change.

Hence, both the legal process and the Warren Court generations had specific reasons to think well of law. And, because law is a "weak" field, it offered little resistance to these generation-specific desires to celebrate and revere law.

Today these generations and their descendants continue to hold their offices and positions. But their generational dreams seem to be over. Legal process has turned out to have serious aesthetic deficiencies; its most significant social achievement has been to pile on transaction costs and to reinforce the barriers to entry to the legal profession. As for the Warren Court—well, it's no longer sitting. And the liberal law review dreams just drift in the ether without a destination or an addressee.

The genres of legal thought associated with legal process and Warren Court normativity are intellectually exhausted. But law (as it is produced by courts) is hardly subservient to intellectual demands. And so what is unreflectively called "law" in our courts and then taught in our classrooms is very often a galloping proceduralism in the service of a messianic normativity (or vice versa).

Still, for all this proliferation of normatively admirable positive law, all is not well. Some legal thinkers are rendered quite anxious in the present moment. "What comes next?" they want to know. "What will be next?" they wonder. "What admirable vision of law will next capture the legal imagination?

Maybe nothing. Maybe what comes next is that we stop treating "law" as something to celebrate, expand, and worship. Maybe, we learn to lay down the law.

NOTES

1. JAMES BOYD WHITE, ACTS OF HOPE CREATING AU-
THORITY IN LITERATURE, LAW AND POLITICS 178 (1995).
2. RONALD DWORKIN, LAW'S EMPIRE 413 (1986).
3. For a discussion of this dual character of the authenticity (or
inauthenticity) of belief, *see* JOSEPH VINING, FROM NEWTON'S
SLEEP 1112 (1995).
4. The distinction between the internal and external perspective has
been a mainstay of much of American legal thought. Here it is rendered
by Professor Ronald Dworkin:

> People who have law make and debate claims about what law
> permits or forbids. . . . This crucial argumentative aspect of legal
> practice can be studied *in two ways* or *from two points of view.* One
> is the *external* point of view of the sociologist or historian. . . . The
> other is the *internal* point of view of those who make the claims.
>
> This book takes up the internal, participants' point of view; it
> tries to grasp the argumentative character of our legal practice by
> joining that practice and struggling with the issues of soundness
> and truth participants face. We will study formal legal argument
> from the judge's viewpoint . . . because judicial argument about
> claims of law is a useful paradigm for exploring the central, propo-

sitional aspect of legal practice. (RONALD DWORKIN, LAWS'S EMPIRE 1314 [1986, emphases added])

See also H. L. A. HART, THE CONCEPT OF LAW 8891 (1961): "[I]t is possible to be concerned with the rules, either merely as an observer who does not accept them, or as a member of the group which accepts and uses them as guides to conduct. We may call these respectively the 'external' and 'internal points of view.' " For a sustained criticism of the distinction and its deployment, see Pierre Schlag, *Normativity and the Politics of Form*, 139 U. PA. L. REV. 801, 916–29 (1991).

5. *See* Edward A. Dauer and Arthur A. Leff, *Correspondence: The Lawyer as Friend*, 86 YALE L. J. 573, 581 (1977).

6. Robert M. Cover, *The Supreme Court, 1982 Term — Foreword: Nomos and Narrative*, 97 Harv. L. Rev. 4 (1983).

7. William Eskridge, *Dynamic Statutory Interpretation*, 135 U. PA. L. REV. 1479, 1483–84, 1506–11 (1987).

8. ANTHONY KRONMAN, THE LOST LAWYER 311–12 (1994).

9. JAMES BOYD WHITE, ACTS OF HOPE CREATING AUTHORITY IN LITERATURE, LAW, AND POLITICS 178 (1994).

10. MARY ANN GLENDON, A NATION UNDER LAWYERS; HOW THE CRISIS IN THE LEGAL PROFESSION IS TRANSFORMING AMERICAN SOCIETY 197–98 (1994).

11. *See* RICHARD POSNER, OVERCOMING LAW (1995); Pierre Schlag, *Law and Phrenology* (unpublished manuscript).

NOTES TO CHAPTER 2

1. [Editor's Note: The editors have been unable to confirm the author's assertion here. The evidence we have suggests that in 1979, the author was employed as an associate with a large law firm in Washington, D.C. The author assures us, however, that the taxi driver/associate distinction is vastly overstated, and in some senses, is actually much more tenuous than might first appear. *Cf.* ELISABETH HYDE, HER NATIVE COLORS 20–37 (1986) (depicting the associate as human resource and information dissemination vehicle).]

2. For further elaboration, see R. G. Lipsey and Kelvin Lancaster,

The General Theory of Second Best, 24 REV. ECON. STUD. 11 (1957).

3. *See, ambivalently,* RONALD DWORKIN, LAW'S EMPIRE (1986).

4. *See, e.g.,* Catharine A. MacKinnon, *Feminism, Marxism, Method and the State: An Agenda for Theory,* 7 SIGNS 515 (1982); Gary Peller, *The Metaphysics of American Law,* 73 CAL. L. REV. 1151 (1985).

5. And the important thing to note is that even as normative legal thought is willing to entertain as a substantive proposition that the notion of an individual humanist subject is an overstatement or a fiction, it will do so only within its own rhetorical form—the very form that tacitly establishes the author and reader as already-constituted autonomous individual subjects.

One of the things that makes normative legal thought's attempts to deal with postmodernism typically uninteresting is that the discussion inevitably comes down to a couple of autonomous individual subjects sitting around talking about whether they exist or not. Not surprisingly, the conclusion is as predictable as it is question-begging. It's like asking God to decide whether Nietzsche is right.

6. And, of course, from the normative perspective, this move seems totally legitimate. It seems totally legitimate because normative legal thought systematically eclipses the rhetorical contributions that its own form makes to its own end products. And thus, not surprisingly, normative legal thought remains unaware of the ways in which it rigs the game.

7. Bambi (Walt Disney Studios 1942).

The Thumper school of jurisprudence, like virtually all other jurisprudential schools, has taken a rather decisive instrumentalist turn lately. Accordingly, in the legal academy, Thumper's transcendental value in niceness has been transformed into the more instrumentalist value in being "constructive." Thus, it is widely held among legal thinkers that one should not merely criticize or destroy, but try to be constructive as well.

I find this sort of position perplexing. Consider a graphic example: If you take someone's neurosis away, are you being *destructive* (of that person's way of doing things) or are you being *constructive* (of a new organically healthy person)? If you were being destructive when you took away the person's neurosis, are you then obliged to do something more afterwards—something constructive? What would this additional constructive moment look like, and how would it help? Indeed, how often does an analysand terminate succesful therapy with the statement, "Yes, I understand I'm fine now. There's just one more question, doctor: What should I do?"

8. *See* Richard Delgado and Jean Stefancic, *Why Do We Tell the Same Stories? Law Reform, Critical Librarianship, and the Triple Helix Dilemma,* 42 STAN. L. REV. 207 (1989) (tracing the disciplinary solipsism of legal thought to the convention-reinforcing character of research indexes and classification systems).

9. *See generally* JOHN RAWLS, A THEORY OF JUSTICE (1971).

10. The only kind of normative legal thought that might actually be having some significant and authentic normative effect on judicial decision-making (and here again, it is difficult to know which way the causal lines would run) is the work of the treatise writers. But this treatise work cannot really be seen as having much effect, since much of it is simply a reflection (an encyclopedic collection) of the modes of thought and norms already extant in the courts.

11. For a provocative discussion of the importance of routine in social interaction, see P. C. Wohlmuth and L. J. Goldberg, *The Significance of Routine in the Operation of Human Regulatory Systems: Reexamining the Relationship of ADR to Law, in Dispute Processing: Legal and Anthropological Perspectives* (B. Aginsky, M. Lowy, V. Rohrl, and D. Wesckstein eds.) (1991).

12. *See* Thomas C. Grey, *Langdell's Orthodoxy,* 45 U. PITT. L. REV. 1, 49–50 (1983).

13. "When unreflective discourse prevails, such as common sense, it is as if the lens has become the world, rather than the portal through which it takes shape." Roger Sherwin, *Dialects and Dominance: A Study of Rhetorical Fields in the Law of Confessions,* 136 U. PA . L. REV. 729, 795 (1988).

> Because ... assumptions and beliefs are internalized as the very grounds of consciousness, they are largely imperceptible to the conscious subject. These conceptualizations are transparent in the sense that they act as a cognitive filter through which the subject sees the social world. As long as the subject remains unreflective, this transparency will project the mutual entailment of the epistemic and the political in a way that will be experienced as "objec-

tive." (Steven L. Winter, *Indeterminacy and Incommensurability in Constitutional Law,* 78 CAL. L. REV. 1441 [1990])

14. And as Derrida cautions, "[T]he simple practice of language ceaselessly reinstates the new terrain on the oldest ground." Jacques Derrida, *The Ends of Man,* in MARGINS OF PHILOSOPHY (A. Bass trans. 1982); *see also* ALASDAIR MACINTYRE, WHOSE JUSTICE? WHICH RATIONALITY? 392–93 (1988).

15. This is why if one seeks to disrupt a disciplinary formalism—normative or otherwise—one cannot simply argue "politely" against it. "Polite" argument is precluded because the very protocol of disciplinary engagement is always already rigged. It has to be: it wouldn't be a discipline if its very form were not already structured so as to preserve the discipline and to derail subversive lines of inquiry. What distinguishes disciplines from mere points of view, sets of ideas, or assortments of theories is that disciplines are linguistically, cognitively, and institutionally entrenched. Disciplines achieve security from challenge by constituting the very self of the disciplinary thinker as a series of rhetorical, cognitive, psychological defenses against troublesome or subversive lines of inquiry. To master or even participate in a discipline is not just to learn an assortment of ideas, techniques, authorities, etc. It is to become a certain kind of thinker, and hence, a certain kind of person.

When a discipline is then challenged (as it is here) disciplinary thinkers are very likely to experience this challenge as an attack on the self—their selves. It is thus not surprising that when disciplinary thinkers are confronted with challenges to their discipline, they react personally and dismissively. They experience challenges as "a way of fighting over whether our lives have been wasted." Calvin Trillin, *A Reporter at Large: Harvard Law,* New Yorker, Mar. 26, 1984, at 53, 83 (quoting a Harvard Law School professor).

This is perfectly understandable. It is also unfortunate.

16. On "ludic" law, see Arthur Leff, *Law And,* 87 YALE L. J. 989, 999 (1978).

17. As Karl Llewelyn put it:

Some institutions . . . have found words and rules serving them as midwife or even as ancestor; but in the main it is action which comes first, to be followed by delayed perception of that action, then by rationalization of the action delayed still longer, and finally by conscious normatization of what has been perceived or rationalized. Before these latter processes have been worked out, the lines of the action commonly have shifted. Veblen's eyes were keen: "A man's ethics are modelled on the conditions of his grandfather's time." (Karl Llewelyn, *The Constitution as an Institution,* 34 COLUM. L. REV. 1, 17 n.30 [1934])

18.

The upshot of Wittgenstein's view of language is that all of our language has meaning only within the language games and "forms of life" in which they are embedded. One must understand the use, the context, the activity, the purpose, the game which is being played. . . . There are many important lessons here for law, but skepticism is not one of them. (Brian Langille, *Revolution without Foundation: The Grammar Scepticism and Law,* 33 MCGILL L. J. 451, 495–96 [1988])

19. On the collapsed Austinian distinction between the performative and the constative, see JOHN LANGSHAW AUSTIN, HOW TO DO THINGS WITH WORDS (1975).

20. This is precisely the point at which traditional legal thinkers voice the fear that judges and other legal actors will impose their own "personal values." At this stage in the degeneration/development of normative legal thought, we are still operating within the fantasy that individual legal thinkers are somehow autonomously in control of their own thoughts and moral values.

21. For an interesting discussion of the relations between the rhetoric and the moral value of our legal terms, see Peter Westen, *"Freedom" and "Coercion"—Virtue Words and Vice Words,* [1985] DUKE L. J. 541, 592.

22. This point of extreme reflexivity is suggested in analogous contexts by Jean Baudrillard when he writes: "And what if all advertising were the apology not of a product but of advertising itself? What if information did not refer back to an event, but to the promotion of information itself as event? What if communication no longer referred back to a message, but to the promotion of communication itself as

myth?" JEAN BAUDRILLARD, LA TRANSPARENCE DU MAL: ESSAI SUR LES PHENOMENES EXTREMES 56 (1990) (1990) (author's translation).

23. ALASDAIR MACINTYRE, AFTER VIRTUE 2 (2d ed. 1984).

24. Still no definitive word on this one.

25. *See* Robert M. Cover, *Violence and the Word*, 95 YALE L. J. 1601 (1986).

26. Yet note, ironically, that this depiction of the situation of legal thought is used recurrently by Stanley Fish—in his characteristically un-congratulatory way—to demonstrate the futility and inadequacy of legal theories.

27. This conceptualization is suggested in Rosemary Coombe's comments on Cover's essay. Rosemary Coombe, *"Same as It Ever Was": Rethinking the Politics of Legal Interpretation*, 34 MCGILL L. J. 601, 649 (1989).

28. (Not me, of course.)

29. HARPER LEE, TO KILL A MOCKINGBIRD (1960).

30. And Stanley Fish is haunting here. In fact here he is saying, "But of course, they'll argue on normative grounds. What else could they do?"

31. *See ex post*, Mark Tushnet, *The Left Critique of Normativity*, 90 MICH. L. REV. 2325 (1992).

32. *See ex post*, ANTHONY KRONMAN, THE LOST LAWYER (1994).

33. *See ex post*, MARY ANN GLENDON, A NATION UNDER LAWYERS: HOW THE CRISIS IN THE LEGAL PROFESSION IS TRANSFORMING AMERICAN SOCIETY (1994).

34. As Baudrillard puts it: "The effects of moral conscience, of collective conscience are entirely mediated effects, and one can read in the therapeutic ardor with which we try to resuscitate this conscience, how little life it retains." J. BAUDRILLARD, *supra* note 22, at 97 (author's translation).

35. *See* MARK KELMAN, A GUIDE TO CRITICAL LEGAL STUDIES (1988).

NOTES TO CHAPTER 3

1. *See* JOHN RAWLS, A THEORY OF JUSTICE (1971).

2. This liberal subject is such a pervasive aesthetic pre-figuration of

American legal thought that its role in the formation of various schools of American legal thought has gone virtually unnoticed. *See* Pierre Schlag, *The Problem of the Subject,* 69 TEX. L. REV. 1627 (1991).

3. Much of this account tracks CHAIM PERELMAN, THE NEW RHETORIC: A TREATISE ON ARGUMENTATION 74–80 (1971).

4. Martha Nussbaum, *Valuing Values: A Case for Reasoned Commitment,* 6 YALE J. L. & HUMAN. 197, 210–15 (1994).

5. *Id.* at 211, 210, 214, 215.

6. *Id.*

7. Ronald K. L. Collins and David M. Skover, *Commerce and Communication,* 71 TEX. L. REV. 697, 708–16 (1993).

8. For a critical discussion of the rhetorical effects of this kind of device (the internal/external perspective) in American legal thought, see Pierre Schlag, *Normativity and the Politics of Form,* 139 U. PA. L. REV. 801, 916–29 (1991).

9. *See* KENNETH BURKE, A GRAMMAR OF MOTIVES 298–301 (1969). "The Romans knew that you could get a god merely by taking an adjective and transforming it into an abstract noun. . . . And particularly, they would detach some attribute from another god, and set it up as a separate divine abstraction. Fides, Libertas, Victoria, Virtus, Felicitas . . ." *Id.* at 301.

10. This is a very rough cut at the conceptualization of relations that are much more complicated and interesting than can be fully described here.

11. Consider this Mobil Oil ad appearing in the *New York Times:*

Imagine yourself and your family swept away from your past life, your job, your home, even your homeland. What you imagine is a reality for millions of people . . . .

The task of resettling the world's dispossessed threatens to overwhelm the international community. Squeezed by financial and political constraints, governments and relief agencies are seeing their resources drained by the scale and complexity of the problem. What can we do as American citizens and corporations?

One answer is to . . . .

MOBIL

(N.Y. Times, May 19, 1988, at A31)

12. *See* Richard Delgado, *Norms and Normal Science: Toward a Critique of Normativity in Legal Thought*, 139 U. PA. L. REV. 933 (1991).

13. I have suggested elsewhere that the value-talk of the legal academy accomplishes very little in the way of realizing its prescriptions. That is not to say that the value-talk of the legal academy is without effect. On the contrary, some of its effects are to idealize and legitimate the activities of courts (whatever they may be doing) and to rehearse an intellectually impoverished and deadening social aesthetic organized around the relatively autonomous subject, and other aesthetic presuppositions associated with rationalist forms of thought.

14. Nussbaum, *supra* note 4, at 216.

15. *Id.* at 217.

16. AMERICAN BAR ASSOCIATION, LEGAL EDUCATION AND PROFESSIONAL DEVELOPMENT: AN EDUCATIONAL CONTINUUM 140 (1992).

17. *Id.* at 213.

18. *See, ironically,* JOHN STUART MILL, ON LIBERTY (1974). In striking contrast to many of his late-twentieth-century academic descendants, this great liberal was keenly aware of the dire results of failing to challenge comfortably held ideas:

> [E]ven if the received opinion be not only true, but the whole truth; unless it is suffered to be, and actually is, vigorously and earnestly contested, it will, by most of those who receive it, be held in the manner of a prejudice, with little comprehension or feeling of its rational grounds. And not only this, but ... the meaning of the doctrine itself will be in danger of being lost or enfeebled, and deprived of its vital effect on the character and conduct; the dogma becoming a mere formal profession, inefficacious for good, but cumbering the ground and preventing the growth of any real *and heartfelt conviction. (Id.* at 116)

NOTES TO CHAPTER 4

1. HANS-GEORG GADAMER, PHILOSOPHICAL HERMENEUTICS 34–35 (David E. Linge trans., 1977).

2. JÜRGEN HABERMAS, THE PHILOSOPHICAL DIS-

COURSE OF MODERNITY: TWELVE LECTURES 286 (Frederick Lawrence trans., 1987).

3. That is: "The text is written so obscurely that you can't figure out exactly what the thesis is (hence *'obscurantisme'*) and then when one criticizes it, the author says, *'Vous m'avez mal compris; vous êtes idiot'* (hence *'terroriste'*)." John R. Searle, *The Word Turned Upside Down*, N.Y. Rev. Books, Oct. 27, 1983, at 74, 77 (reviewing JONATHAN CULLER, ON DECONSTRUCTION: THEORY AND CRITICISM AFTER STRUCTURALISM [1983]).

4. Jacques Derrida, *Three Questions to Hans-Georg Gadamer,* in DIALOGUE AND DECONSTRUCTION: THE GADAMER-DERRIDA ENCOUNTER 52, 53 (Diane P. Michelfelder and Richard E. Palmer eds., 1989).

5. JEAN-FRANÇOIS LYOTARD, THE DIFFEREND 9–10 (Georges Van Den Abbeele trans., 1990).

6. Lyotard writes:

There is a differend, therefore, concerning the means of establishing reality between the partisans of agonistics and the partisans of dialogue. How can this differend be regulated? Through dialogue, say the latter; through the agôn, say the former. To stick to this, the differend would only perpetuate itself, becoming a sort of meta-differend, a differend about the way to regulate the differend about the way to establish reality. (*Id.* at 26)

7. Gadamer writes:

A person who is trying to understand a text is always performing an act of projecting. He projects before himself a meaning for the text as a whole as soon as some initial meaning emerges in the text. Again, the latter emerges only because he is reading the text with particular expectations in regard to a certain meaning. The working out of this fore-project, which is constantly revised in terms of what emerges as he penetrates into the meaning, is understanding what is there. (HANS-GEORG GADAMER, TRUTH AND METHOD 236 [Garret Barden and John Cumming trans., 2d ed. 1975])

8. Gadamer writes:

The circle, then, is not formal in nature, it is neither subjective nor objective, but describes understanding as the interplay of the movement of tradition and the movement of the interpreter. The anticipation of meaning that governs our understanding of a text is not an act of subjectivity, but proceeds from the communality that binds us to the tradition. But this is contained in our relation to tradition, in the constant process of education. Tradition is not simply a precondition into which we come, but we produce it ourselves, inasmuch as we understand, participate in the evolution of tradition and hence further determine it ourselves. Thus the circle of understanding is not a "methodological" circle, but describes an ontological structural element in understanding. (*Id.* at 261)

9. Lyotard, *supra* note 5, at 13.

10. Gadamer, *supra* note 7, at 238–39.

11. *See generally* Pierre Schlag, *Normativity and the Politics of Form*, 139 U. PA, L. REV. 801 (1991).

12. *See generally* Pierre Schlag, *The Problem of the Subject*, 69 TEX. L. REV. 1627 (1991); Steven L. Winter, *Indeterminacy and Incommensurability in Constitutional Law*, 78 CAL. L. REV. 1443 (1990).

13. Habermas writes:

Communicative action takes place within a lifeworld that remains at the backs of participants in communication. It is present to them only in the prereflective form of taken-for-granted background assumptions and naively mastered skills. (1 JÜRGEN HABERMAS, THE THEORY OF COMMUNICATIVE ACTION 335 [Thomas McCarthy trans., 1984])

14. Gadamer writes:

We are always within the situation, and to throw light on it is a task that is never entirely completed. This is true also of the hermeneutic situation, i.e. the situation in which we find ourselves with regard to the tradition that we are trying to understand. The illumination of this situation—effective-historical reflection—can never be completely achieved, but this is not due to a lack in the reflection, but lies in the essence of the historical being which is ours. (Gadamer, *supra* note 7, at 269)

15. Foucault writes:

Expressing their thoughts in words of which they are not the masters, enclosing them in verbal forms whose historical dimensions they are unaware of, men believe that their speech is their servant and do not realize that they are submitting themselves to its demands. The grammatical arrangements of a language are the *a priori* of what can be expressed in it. (MICHEL FOUCAULT, THE ORDER OF THINGS 297 [1970])

16. Derrida writes:

[O]ne cannot do anything, least of all speak, without determining (in a manner that is not only theoretical, but practical and performative) a context. Such experience is always political because it implies, insofar as it involves determination, a certain type of non-"natural" relationship to others. . . . Once this generality and this a priori structure have been recognized, the question can be raised, not whether a politics is implied (it always is), but which politics is implied in such a practice of contextualization. This you can then go on to analyze, but you cannot suspect it, much less denounce it except on the basis of another contextual determination every bit as political. (Jacques Derrida, *Afterword: Toward an Ethic of Discussion*, in LIMITED INC. 111, 136 [Samuel Weber trans., 1988])

17. Lyotard writes: "Nothing can be said about *reality* that does not presuppose it" (Lyotard, *supra* note 5, at 32, emphasis added).
18. Edward L. Rubin, *On Beyond Truth: A Theory for Evaluating Legal Scholarship*, 80 CAL. L. REV. 889, 900 (1992) (emphasis added).
19. *Id.* at 895 (emphasis added).
20. *Id.* at 910 (emphasis added).

21. *See* Steven L. Winter, *Bull Durham and the Uses of Theory*, 42 STAN. L. REV. 639, 686–87 (1990).

22. Rubin, *supra* note 18, at 895 (emphasis added).

23. *Id.* at 892 (emphasis added).

24. *Id.* at 900 (emphasis added).

25. *Id.*

26. *Id. See generally* STANLEY FISH, DOING WHAT COMES NATURALLY: CHANGE, RHETORIC AND THE PRACTICE OF THEORY IN LITERARY AND LEGAL STUDIES (1989).

27. Rubin, *supra* note 18, at 903–4 (footnote omitted).

28. *See generally* Schlag, *supra* note 11.

29. *See generally* Schlag, *supra* note 12.

30. For elaboration, see Schlag, *supra* note 11, at 808–11.

31. But it is in question. *Symposium, The Critique of Normativity*, 139 U. PA. L. REV. 801–1075 (1991).

32. *Cf.* JOSEPH VINING, THE AUTHORITATIVE AND THE AUTHORITARIAN (1986).

33. Rubin, *supra* note 18, at 904 (emphasis added).

34. *Id.*

35. ROBERTO M. UNGER, FALSE NECESSITY (1987).

36. RONALD DWORKIN, LAW'S EMPIRE vii (1986).

37. *See* Schlag, *supra* note 12, at 1732–36 (describing the Langdellian paradigm of the legal thinker).

38. Robert M. Cover, *The Supreme Court, 1982 Term—Foreword: Nomos and Narrative*, 97 HARV. L. REV. 4, 53 (1983).

39. Roberto M. Unger, *The Critical Legal Studies Movement*, 96 HARV. L. REV. 561, 674–75 (1983); Pierre Schlag, *"Le Hors de Texte, C'est Moi": The Politics of Form and the Domestication of Deconstruction*, 11 CARDOZO L. REV. 1631 (1990).

40. GEORG W. F. HEGEL, THE PHENOMENONOLOGY OF MIND 79 (J. Baillie trans., 2d ed. 1949).

Notes to Chapter 5

1. Manuscripts on file with the author's attorney.

2. *See supra* note 1.

3. *See, e.g.,* Posner, *The Decline of Law as an Autonomous Discipline, 1962–1987*, 100 HARV. L. REV. 761 (1987).

4. *See, ironically, id.* at 766–69, 778.

5. *See generally* Vining, *Law and Enchantment: The Place of Belief,* 86 MICH. L. REV. 577 (1987).

6. A number of commentators from varying perspectives have recognized the degradation of the legal mind into mindless bureaucratic repetition of sterile legal forms. *See, e.g., id.;* James Boyd White, *Intellectual Integration,* 82 NW. U. L. REV. 1, 5–6 (1987); Robert Nagel, *The Formulatic Constitution,* 84 MICH. L. REV. 165 (1985); David Kennedy, *Critical Theory, Structuralism and Contemporary Legal Scholarship,* 21 NEW ENG. L. REV. 209, 211 (1986).

7. RONALD DWORKIN, LAW'S EMPIRE 274 (1986).

8. Actually, our conceptions of subject-object relations (both conscious and preconscious) are much more varied than this quick description indicates. For an excellent discussion of the role of metaphor in legal thought, see Steven Winter, *Transcendental Nonsense, Metaphoric Reasoning, and the Cognitive Stakes for Law,* 137 U. PA. L. REV. 1105 (1989).

9. *See* Stanley Fish, *Fish v. Fiss,* 36 STAN. L. REV. 1325 (1984).

10. RICHARD POSNER, ECONOMIC ANALYSIS OF LAW 12–13 (1986).

11. *See* Ronald Dworkin, *Law's Ambition for Itself,* 71 VA. L. REV. 173, 177 (1985). For an elaboration of the theme in the text, see James Boyle, *Legal Fiction (Book Review),* 38 HAST. L. REV. 1013 (1987).

12. O. W. HOLMES, COLLECTED LEGAL PAPERS 238 (1921).

13. O. W. HOLMES, THE COMMON LAW 1 (1881).

14. W. JAMES, ESSAYS IN PRAGMATISM 141 (1948).

NOTES TO CHAPTER 6

1. DAVID LODGE, SMALL WORLD 29–30 (1984).

2. Stanley Fish, *Dennis Martinez and the Uses of Theory,* 96 YALE L. J. 1773, 1795–96 (1987) [hereinafter Fish, *Uses of Theory*].

3. STANLEY FISH, IS THERE A TEXT IN THIS CLASS? 14 (1980) [hereinafter Fish, *Text in This Class*]; Stanley Fish, *Fish v. Fiss,* 36 STAN. L. REV. 1325, 1332 (1984) [hereinafter Fish, *Fish v. Fiss*].

4. Fish considers nihilism an untenable, impossible position steeped

in bad metaphysics, see Fish, *Fish v. Fiss, supra* note 3, at 1333–34, 1346.

5. *See* Fish, *Fish v. Fiss, supra* note 3, at 1326–27.

6. *See* Fish, *Working on the Chain Gang: Interpretation in Law and Literature,* 60 TEX. L. REV. 551, 564–65 (1982); Fish, *Uses of Theory, supra* note 2, at 1781.

7. Fish, *Fish v. Fiss, supra* note 3, at 1326.

8. Fish, *Consequences,* in AGAINST THEORY: LITERARY STUDIES AND THE NEW PRAGMATISM 106, 124–25 (W. J. T. Mitchell ed. 1985) [hereinafter Fish, *Consequences*].

9. Fish, *Uses of Theory, supra* note 2, at 1785–90.

10. *Id.* at 1781–83.

11. *Id.* at 1794–95.

12. Fish, *Fish v. Fiss, supra* note 3, at 1326.

13. Fish, *Fish v. Fiss, supra* note 3, at 1326.

14. *Cf.* DOUGLAS R. HOFSTADTER, GÖDEL, ESCHER AND BACH 17–18 (1979) (exploring Gödel's theorem, which suggests that "all consistent axiomatic formulations of number theory include undecidable propositions").

For an analogue of the theorem in the legal context, see David Kennedy, *The Turn to Interpretation,* 58 S. CAL. L. REV. 251, 257 (1985).

15. Michael Moore, *A Natural Law Theory of Interpretation,* 58 S. CAL. L. REV. 277, 322–28 (1985).

16. Fish, *Uses of Theory, supra* note 2, at 1782.

17. RONALD DWORKIN, TAKING RIGHTS SERIOUSLY 87–88 (1977).

18. Fish, *Uses of Theory, supra* note 2, at 1787–94.

19. *Id.* at 1795–96.

20. Fish, *Fish v. Fiss, supra* note 3, at 1326; Fish, *Uses of Theory, supra* note 2, at 1783–85, 1793–95, 1797.

21. Fish, *Text in This Class, supra* note 3, at 14; Fish, *Fish v. Fiss, supra* note 3, at 1327; Fish, *Uses of Theory, supra* note 2, at 1797. For an early complaint that Fish has left his concept of "interpretive communities" rather vague and undetermined, see Scholes, *Who Cares about the Text?* 17 NOVEL: A FORUM ON FICTION 171, 173–75 (Winter 1984).

22. Fish, *Consequences, supra* note 8, at 111–12.

23. And not unreasonably, Fish has been interpreted in just this way. McCormick, *Swimming Upstream with Stanley Fish,* 44 J. AESTHETICS & ART CRITICISM 67, 72–73 (1985). Accordingly, Fish has been attacked for proposing precisely that which he says is not possible: a theory of interpretation. Knapp and Michaels, *Against Theory,* in AGAINST THEORY, *supra* note 8, at 11, 28–30. At other times, however, Fish seems to use the term "interpretive communities" merely as a code name for that which we cannot make articulate, but which surely must exist if there is (and if there is to be) some stability, some regularity in the way in which we describe the world. Fish, *Fish v. Fiss, supra* note 3, at 1327–28.

24. Drucilla Cornell, *"Convention" and Critique,* 7 CARDOZO L. REV. 679, 689–91 (1986).

25. Fish's thesis has been criticized on the grounds that its totalitarian thrust deprives the individual interpreter of freedom and power and fails to account for intracommunity disagreements, Scholes, *supra* note 21, at 171–73.

26. And just so that there is no misunderstanding, I would agree with Zapp on this point.

27. As one commentator has noted:

> [A]lthough communal conventions circumscribe the available options for interpretive practice, Fish leaves it to individuals to decide on the actual pattern (or chaos) of choices. Far from burying individuals, Fish has reinstated them in their role as the prime and privileged makers of meaning and history. Posing as a radical determinist, he stands revealed as a closet humanist. (Allan Hutchinson, *Part of an Essay on Power and Interpretation [With Suggestions on How to Make Bouillabaise],* 60 N.Y.U. L. REV. 850, 870 [1985])

28. *See generally* JEAN PAUL SARTRE, BEING AND NOTHINGNESS (H. Barnes trans. 1966).

29. *See generally* B. F. SKINNER, BEYOND FREEDOM AND DIGNITY (1971).

30. Fish, *Text in This Class, supra* note 3, at 180, 321, 368–69 (emphasis in original).

31. Fish, *Fish v. Fiss, supra* note 3, at 1332; Fish, *Consequences, supra* note 8, at 111–12; Fish, *Uses of Theory, supra* note 2, at 1788–90; Fish, *Text in This Class, supra* note 3, at 170–73.

32. The earliest use of the term "grok" I have found is in R. HEIN-LEIN, STRANGER IN A STRANGE LAND (1961).

33. Fish, *Text in This Class, supra* note 3, at 335.

34. Fish might say that the relatively autonomous self does not need a reason to privilege itself. It just does. Right again: it just does . . . until . . . of course, it doesn't.

35. In fact, I think "wrong" has been given a bum rap. It has its uses. *See* Schlag, *The Brilliant, the Curious and the Wrong,* 39 STAN. L. REV. 917, 923 n.18 (1987).

36. David Lodge, *supra* note 1, at 33.

37. Sure, every decoding is another encoding. But if one takes Zapp's axiom seriously, it turns out to be the other way around: every encoding is another decoding.

38. Oh sure, there are other available conceptions of self (but none so encompassing nor so modern). Other options include, for instance, the more ancient *fully autonomous self*—which knows no limits at all in its ability to adjudicate the nature of reality. This is the sort of self that not only believes in *but also knows* the absolute truth. In the modern world, you often find these kinds of selves serving as prophets (minor or major) in any of the available fundamentalist/foundationalist schools of thought. There is also the more recent *ironic self.* This is the sort of self that revels in the dissonance and inconsistencies of the modern world, insisting over and over again (very systematically) that the concept of the coherent self is vastly overrated. One could go on and on.

39. Fish, *Uses of Theory, supra* note 2, at 1773–74 (quoting N.Y. Times, June 26, 1985, at B13, col. 1).

40. LUDWIG WITTGENSTEIN, PHILOSOPHICAL INVES-TIGATIONS I 241 (G. Anscombe trans. 3d ed. 1958). For a comparison of Fish and Wittgenstein, see Cornell, *supra* note 24, at 684–91 (1986); Dasenbrock, *Accounting for the Changing Certainties of Interpretive Communities,* 101(5) M.L.N. 1022 (Dec. 1986). The account Fish offers is similar to Wittgenstein's arguments, but only up to a point.

41. Fish, *Text in This Class, supra* note 3, at 305–9; Fish, *Uses of Theory, supra* note 2, at 1773–79.

42. Fish, *Uses of Theory, supra* note 2, at 1779.

43. The only thing that might actually work in the sentence would be "God" or analogous terms—i.e., precisely those terms that signify something outside or beyond human experience.

44. Fish, *Uses of Theory, supra* note 2, at 1779.

45. And Fish knows this: he tries mightily to avoid ever saying anything about the limits, jurisdiction, edge, contour, or perimeter of his "interpretive communities." And should you invest the term "interpretive community" with some actual concrete boundaries (e.g., Harvard Law School, the Supreme Court, legal academia, California)—well, that is something you will have done to Fish's text, something that he can always already disavow.

46. Fish, *Uses of Theory, supra* note 2, at 1774.

47. Berkow, *The Old and New Manager,* N.Y. Times, June 26, 1985, at B13, col. 1. Maybe Weaver was out of practice. But if so, that's just bad theory.

Notes to Chapter 7

1. Stanley Fish, *Fraught with Death: Skepticism, Progressivism, and the First Amendment,* 64 U. COLO. L. REV. 1061 (1993).

2. Ronald Dworkin, *Law's Ambitions for Itself,* 71 VA. L. REV. 173 (1985).

3. As a scholar of speech-act theory and the work of Austin, Stanley Fish, of course, was prepared to recognize this all along. JOHN LANGSHAW AUSTIN, HOW TO DO THINGS WITH WORDS 145–47 (1989). In turn, all of this was previously known—one way or another—to Wittgenstein and Nietzsche, and . . . in short, the contamination reaches very far back.

4. THOMAS I. EMERSON, TOWARD A GENERAL THEORY OF THE FIRST AMENDMENT 17 (1966) (action/expression).

5. United States v. O'Brien, 391 U.S. 367 (1968).

6. John Hart Ely, *Comment, Flag Desecration: A Case Study in the Roles of Categorization and Balancing in First Amendment Analysis,* 88 HARV. L. REV. 1482, 1495 (1975).

7. In Professor Ely's footnote, it is the entire expression/action dichotomy (without limitation) that is found wanting:

The expression-action distinction is by no means all there is to Professor Emerson's theory of the first amendment. His sensitive explication of the values underlying that amendment cannot be ignored by anyone who would try to understand it. The impulse to define clear categories, and thus better to safeguard freedom of expression in times of national panic, is also one I share. *I simply do not think this distinction can be made to work.* (Ely, *supra* note 6, at 1495 n.53, emphasis added, citation omitted)

8. But it is. *See* Pierre Schlag, *Cannibal Moves: An Essay on the Metamorphoses of the Legal Distinction,* 40 STAN. L. REV. 929 (1988).

9. That's why they are presented elsewhere. *See elsewhere* Pierre Schlag, *Clerks in the Maze,* 91 MICH. L. REV. 2053 (1993) (discussing the answers).

10. For a description of Zeno's paradox, see 2 W. K. C. GUTHRIE, A HISTORY OF GREEK PHILOSOPHY 91–93 (1965).

11. I don't want to suggest that liberalism is *particularly* deficient in having such a problem. All offspring of the enlightenment have this problem. Indeed, Marxists have had sustained difficulties dealing with a homologous paradox. For Marxists, the same problem makes its appearance in the question having to do with the coming to consciousness of the proletariat. The proletariat, of course, is the universal class, the agent of history. What happens when it doesn't realize its historical mission, or worse, it becomes politically regressive? It is this sort of anxious question that triggers the entire dialectic of Marxian argument (including the disagreements of Lenin and Rosa Luxemburg) about the nature of class consciousness, the proper role of the vanguard party, voluntarism, and so on.

12. Fish, *supra* note 1, at 1062.

13. *Id.*

14. *Id.*

15. On "theory" and "critical self-consciousness," see STANLEY FISH, DOING WHAT COMES NATURALLY: CHANGE, RHETORIC AND THE PRACTICE OF THEORY IN LITERARY AND LEGAL STUDIES 372–98, 436–70 (1989). On "liberalism," see Stanley Fish, *Liberalism Doesn't Exist* [1987] DUKE L. J. 997.

16. It too is self-consuming, you understand.

17. Fish, *supra* note 1, at 1083.

NOTES TO CHAPTER 8

1. Here is the internal perspective, as rendered by Professor Ronald Dworkin:

> People who have law, make and debate claims about what law permits or forbids. . . . This crucial argumentative aspect of legal practice can be studied *in two ways* or *from two points of view.* One is the *external* point of view of the sociologist or historian. . . . The other is the *internal* point of view of those who make the claims. . . .
>
> This book takes up the internal, participants' point of view; it tries to grasp the argumentative character of our legal practice by joining that practice and struggling with the issues of soundness and truth participants face. We will study formal legal argument from the judge's viewpoint . . . because judicial argument about claims of law is a useful paradigm for exploring the central, propositional aspect of legal practice. (RONALD DWORKIN, LAW'S EMPIRE 13–14 [1986], emphasis added)

2. For my elaboration of some of these difficulties, see Pierre Schlag, *Normativity and the Politics of Form,* 139 U. PA. L. REV. 801, 916–26 (1991).

3. This argument is developed at greater length in Pierre Schlag, *"Le Hors de Texte, C'est Moi": The Politics of Form and the Domestication of Deconstruction,* 11 CARDOZO L. REV. 1631 (1990).

4. *See* Pierre Schlag, *Law and Phrenology* (unpublished manuscript).

5. *Id.*

6. GEORG HEGEL, THE PHENOMENOLOGY OF MIND 79 (J. B. Baillie, trans. 1967).

7. *See* Pierre Schlag, *Rights in the Postmodern Condition* in THE PHILOSOPHICAL AND SOCIAL FOUNDATIONS OF RIGHTS (Tom Kearns and Austin Sarat eds., forthcoming).

8. *See* Paul F. Campos, *Secular Fundamentalism,* 94 COLUM. L. REV. 1814 (1994).

9. As Roberto Unger put it:

The legal academy that we entered dallied in one more variant of the perennial effort to restate power and preconception as right. ... Having failed to persuade themselves of all but the most equivocal versions of the inherited creed, they nevertheless clung to its implications and brazenly advertised their own failure as the triumph of worldly wisdom over intellectual and political enthusiasm. History they degraded into the retrospective rationalization of events. Philosophy they abased into an inexhaustible compendium of excuses for the truncation of legal analysis. The social sciences they perverted into the source of argumentative ploys with which to give arbitrary though stylized policy discussions the blessing of a specious authority.

When we came, they were like a priesthood that had lost their faith and kept their jobs. (Roberto M. Unger, *The Critical Legal Studies Movement*, 96 HARV. L. REV. 561, 674–75 [1983])

10. *See* Paul F. Campos, *Advocacy and Scholarship*, 81 CAL. L. REV. 817 (1993).

Notes to Chapter 9

1. Robert M. Cover, *Violence and the Word*, 95 YALE L. J. 1601 (1986).

2. *Id.*

3. FRIEDRICH NIETZSCHE, THE GENEALOGY OF MORALS, Second Essay, Section 1 at 58 (Trans. Walter Kaufman 1989).

4. *Id.* Second Essay, section 3 at 62.

5. *Id.*

6. Nietzsche writes:

It was in this sphere then, the sphere of legal obligations, that the moral conceptual world of "guilt" "conscience," "duty" "sacredness of duty" had its origin: its beginnings were like the beginnings of everything great on earth, soaked in blood thoroughly and for a long time. And might one not add that, fundamentally, this world has never since lost a certain odor of blood and torture? (*Id.* Second Essay, section 6 at 65)

7. *Id.* Second essay, Section 11 at p. 75.

8. No doubt, as in other fields what the law does not recognize, does not understand, it generally does not "treat" very well.

9. When Charles Reich wrote about this process in "The New Property," he was seeking to counsel recognition of the new forms of property already created by the State. Charles Reich, *The New Property,* 73 YALE L. J. 733 (1964).

10. To say that these are merely figurative or metaphorical expressions is, in one sense, true. But the question then becomes: these are figurative or metaphorical expressions of what? If the "what" here is nothing, then it cannot provide a source of meaning. Conversely, if the "what" is a meaning-originating source, we are back to animism.

11. This identification with the figure of the judge disintegrates to various extents among practicing lawyers. It is largely in response to the disintegration of this identification (and the attendant corruption of a "pure" vision of law) that some legal academics resist hiring candidates who have had "too much" practice experience.

12. Pierre Schlag, *Clerks in the Maze,* 91 MICH. L. REV. 2053, 2055 (1993).

13. *See generally* DUNCAN KENNEDY, LEGAL EDUCATION AND THE REPRODUCTION OF HIERARCHY: A POLEMIC AGAINST THE SYSTEM (1983).

14. Now, at the level of the individual, this is tragic. But at the social level, one can see how this sort of training might be good for legal practice. Such an impartation of cognitive deficits—Veblen called this "trained incapacity"—would produce a class of persons, the legally educated, who could be counted upon to read legally significant texts and events in the same highly delimited, routinized, that is to say, predictable manner. Similarly, this capacity would facilitate essential social and economic functions of communication and memory.

INDEX

* 9 7 8 0 8 1 4 7 8 0 5 4 1 *